Out to Pasture

The Boomer's Guide to Life After Fifty

Terry Killinger

To mom with love enjoy!

Copyright © 2017 Terry Killinger
and cover art licensors.
Cover Photography: Cheryl Flaim

All rights reserved.
No part of this publication may be reproduced, stored in a retrieval system, or transmitted in any form or by any means without the prior written permission of the publisher.

ISBN-10: 1544977352
ISBN-13: 978-1544977355

*To Mom with Love
Enjoy!*

DEDICATION

To Charme, my wife of over forty years. The love of my life, and editor in chief. Always a rich source of ideas and consternation.

ACKNOWLEDGMENTS

Special thanks to our great kids Cheryl, Lisa and Joe, and our grandkids Caleb, Eli, Jorie, and Lucas. To Colleen and Paul; Val and Bert; Carrie and Jade; Jen, Dan and Jack; and to the rest of the Downtown Denizens.

CONTENTS

	Boom	1
	Out to Pasture	3

Part 1 - Still Working

1	Hunters and Gatherers	9
2	Time Tested Work Strategies	15
3	Playing Well with Others	19
4	I.T. - The Fist of God	25
5	If Only	29

Part 2 - Transition and Transformation

6	Last Day	35
7	Re-Emergence – Now What?	39

Downsizing

8	Your New Home	43
9	Your New Roof	47
10	Your New Water Heater	51

Pest Control

11	Regarding Bats	59
12	Ants Go Marching	63
13	Relatives	69

The New Millennium

14	Technology's Bitch	75

Part 3 - Boom Time

Travel

15	Best Places	83
16	Getting There is Half the Fun	89
17	About Wine	95

Pets

18	Your First Ferret	101
19	About Dogs	105
20	About Cats	111

Activities

21	Quilting	117
22	Deer Hunting (Inadvertent)	123
23	A Guide to Lawn Care	127
24	Everything but the Squeal	137
25	A Shop on a Different Corner	145
26	Understanding Professional Football	151

Part 4 - Legacy: The Grandkids

27	Early Onset Grandparent Syndrome	163
28	The Pinewood Derby	169
29	An Ode to Black Friday	175
30	Let There be Light	177
31	Some Assembly Required	183
32	The Day Trip	187
33	The One That Got Away	193
34	Take It From the Top	203

| 35 | Watch This! | 211 |
| 36 | Did I Do That? | 219 |

Part 5 - The Pasture

37	The Art of Getting Old	229
38	I See Dead People	235
39	How to Live Forever	243
40	Simpler Times	251
41	Ever After	255

Appendix

| Principal Boomer Activity Chart | 261 |
| About the Author | 263 |

Boom

The captain of the massive transport ship gripped the railing as if his life, and the lives of the hundreds of troops on board, depended on it. The war had been won and they were on their way back home. The storm was giving them an unwelcome reminder that they were not back with their loved ones just yet.

After all that they had been through, the last thing they needed was to have to endure gale force winds and high seas. The crew had been made aware of the conditions before they had set sail, but they had no intention of waiting to get back home with their heroic cargo.

For the next several hours waves crashed over the bow as the vessel relentlessly drove forward across the Atlantic. This was nothing, the smallest of inconveniences, compared to what the stoic passengers and crew had already experienced.

And then, as if the heavens understood, the skies began to clear in the west. The brave warriors and shipmates on board were seasick to a person, except the captain, of course. He didn't have time for that. He was bringing his victors home.

Finally, the voyage was nearing its end. After far too long enduring the storm, with little to do but watch the whitecaps, count the circling gulls, chatter at the dolphins playing just off the side of the ship, and reminisce about how things were before the war, their destination was finally visible in the distance.

The fierce rain and wind had long since subsided, and they could see the actual landing pier that glistened as a welcoming mist covered dot on the dark line of land just at the edge of the curving horizon.

Thousands of grateful and excited well wishers were on the pier, waiting for their loved ones to return. They had waited a long time indeed.

Most of the crowd were what we now call the significant others of the heroes on board, and they waved, shouted, and clapped as the ship neared the shore.

The war was over, and we had won. As the gangplank was finally lowered and the passengers disembarked into the arms of their waiting sweethearts, everyone knew that the great *Boom*, from which we are all descendents, was about to begin.

It was the end of a dangerous and serious time in the world. The future held the promise of a period in which everyone could pause, and even have a little fun again.

It is in this spirit that we offer a few not so serious thoughts for those of you who are now part of the population that has been awkwardly christened The Baby Boom Generation. We are here to help you navigate your way through the relentless aging process that has introduced itself to your minds and middles.

We are speaking of the time in which the youngest of our heroes' children from that challenging era have recently turned the big Five-O.

Welcome to the time in which each Boomer is looking directly into the cackling, leering specter of...

...life after fifty.

Out to Pasture

Are you a Boomer? Those who are have lived through a unique and important time in history. Without getting into a lot of detail, suffice it to say that when you were growing up there were only three television channels, and all of them went off the air each night before midnight. You were then rewarded with a rousing rendition of the national anthem, followed by that disturbing circle image, followed by fuzz.

This book is specifically designed to guide you smoothly and successfully through the rest of your life. It utilizes anecdotal vignettes and allegories to march each of you through the complex stages of your evolution into becoming a card carrying Boomer, and beyond.

Yes, we realize now that it may have worked better if we actually knew what anecdotal vignettes and allegories were before we started, but that ship has long since sailed.

Together, we will walk through the various experiences and circumstances that most Boomers are now encountering, beginning with the unfortunate situation involving the fact that most of you still have to work for a living.

It is clearly understood that there may be a few of you who will question the reasoning behind our taking on this important task.

You may even be thinking, *Who gave you the job of telling us what to do in our old age anyway, pal? I am way too young to be thinking about retirement. In any case, I couldn't stop working even if I wanted.* In the real world people just don't retire anymore until they can't hear the manager shouting for them to get back to work.

Excellent questions to be sure. The harsh truth is if you are of Boomer age, you are getting somewhat oldish at this point, even if you didn't want it to happen.

Whether or not you aspire to, or are forced to, continue working until you are ninety (the new seventy-nine they say), go ahead and admit that you have thought about not having to work for The Man anymore. Go ahead. Admit it.

For those of you seeking to address the validity of our credentials, please refer to page thirty-one, paragraph sixteen, of the Legal Addendum which is on file in the basement of the Bismarck, North Dakota Town Hall.

In that document it is clear that a staff member of one of the universities (in the East, we think), provided what we have interpreted to mean permission to advise you on everything that you will want to do from this point forward with your life.

Many Boomers have already made the transition into the scenario that all managers in major corporations simply call being put out to pasture.

Some pundits have begun calling this inevitable transition as moving from your old work into your new work. Maybe it should actually be referred to as moving from your old life into your older life. Either way, you now have a great opportunity to live life differently than you did for all of those years before, when you were struggling to make your mark on the world.

It was the time when you somehow started and maintained a relationship that lasted long enough to produce off-spring, immediately followed by the need to feed many people every day, pay for something described as orthodontia, attend hip-hop dance recitals, and post bail.

Unless you have somewhere else to be that is really important, why not take a stroll with us down your future memory lane via the anecdotal experiences outlined in this speculative tome.

Together we will discuss at length what will surely happen to you during your transition into, and the subsequent journey through, your Boomer years. We will also cover what you could have done to make it work far better if you had read and acted upon the sage and often correctly spelled advice offered here.

Welcome to *The Pasture*.

Part 1

Still Working

1

Hunters and Gatherers

The hunters of the tribe had just left the village. Each warrior sported an impressive spear with glistening obsidian blades and markings of big dead animals on the shafts. The large group sang robustly as they ran to the jungle below. They belted out *Working for the Weekend* with their enthusiastic voices, carrying the sound far out into the valley, reverberating off the hills, and driving the origin of that particular song back several millennia. Ironically, the alerted and frightened wildlife scattered in every direction for miles.

The hunt was going well until the incident. They had cornered and pinned an unlucky mastodon against the cliff wall just like it said to do in the manual. Apparently Grog had failed to read page twelve, which focused on getting too close. The resulting carnage was hideous to observe after the giant beast slipped on some vegetation and sat down with a grunt on the unfortunate warrior.

To be clear, without diminishing the tragedy, Grog had been involved in previous situations that had landed him on long term probation with the team. Usually on the hunts, he was relegated to the back of the line, carrying the dried snake snacks, vitamin water, and Skittles for the other warriors. Some of the hunters had quietly commented that he appeared to have gatherer written all over him, but the chief still held out a faint hope.

In fact, twice in the last month Grog had become distracted by another lizard or monkey, taken a wrong turn, fallen into another large crater, and had subsequently required reluctant and eventual rescuing.

One day, in his anxiety to achieve recognition as a great hunter, Grog had stolen out of the camp in the night. He had inadvertently made his way over the far ridge, to the village of the tribe's enemies known as the Mean People.

He hadn't intended it, of course. He had only wanted to go out on his own, find and skewer some large opportunistic meat source for the village, and consequently be worshiped as a hero, maybe even being elevated to head warrior. But his tracking skills failed him once again and he ended up just outside the rival tribe's pet feeding area.

Grog probably should have noticed that the half dozen cute sheep were housed in a small wooden pen, and that each animal had a name plaque near its straw sleeping area. Unfortunately, he did not. After several wide shots and a near miss, he finally bagged his first kill. The sign above the still twitching animal said, in the standard tribal language, Sacred Home of Bambi - Beloved Spirit Guide of the Chief. Sadly, Grog had never really paid much attention in the learn to read at the fire sessions. You see, there was this girl.

It had taken him nearly a full day to drag the small carcass a mile and a half back toward his village, although it only weighed about five pounds. The relentless beating drums and barking dogs had begun long ago, emanating from the rival tribe's village location. *Hmmm*, he pondered, *I wonder what all that ruckus is about?*

Not long after that, several hundred enemy warriors intercepted Grog, who had apparently once again fallen into one of the craters and was yelling wildly to be saved. With the crater rim lined with fierce hunters pounding their chests and shaking their spears emblazoned with images of large beasts, the situation appeared dire.

But amazingly, just before the frenzied warriors were about the turn the inept mutton thief into a large pin cushion, there was a faint "baaahhh" at the back of the crater. The enemy chief, who had accompanied his men to exact revenge on, first Grog, and then his village, suddenly shouted loudly for his men to halt.

"Baaaahhh," once again was heard bleating nearby.

As it turns out, Grog had only slightly stunned the sheep in his ill-fated attempt to capture dinner for the tribe. The enemy chief paused as he stood over the failed hunter. After standing several minutes with his entire tribe around him in a circle shouting, "Gut thief...slowly," the chief threw down his spear. *What an idiot*, he decided as he picked up Bambi and led his warriors back to their village over the ridge, avoiding what was sure to have been a massacre of Grog's entire tribe.

With head down in defeat, the would be provider climbed out of the crater and slowly began walking back home. An upbeat "baaahhhh" could once again be faintly heard from beyond the ridge.

Later that day, Grog finally made his way back home. No one had actually noticed that he was gone, and he never mentioned the incident to anyone. He did vow to start attending the learn to read sessions, but couldn't remember where the fire pit was located, and soon forgot about the idea entirely.

The hunt in which Grog met his demise hadn't gone well, for Grog at least. For a while it appeared that the warriors might have to return to the village empty handed. But the area was quite slick after the incident. In the end, the mastodon that had inadvertently sat upon the diminutive buffoon also slipped and broke its neck on a rock.

The brave warriors were enthusiastically welcomed as they returned triumphantly to the waiting village with meat for several days, some of which presumably included parts of the former Grog. Oh well.

Much later, one of the village women looked up briefly from her gathering project and mused, *I wonder what ever happened to that Grog guy?* She then quickly forgot about it and went back to work rubbing dried cactus between two large rocks. Meanwhile, the village ate well for many days.

In the modern world, the disciplines first developed by our ancestors' tribal cultures still persist. The multitudes of Boomers who are still working face the same laws of the jungle each day as they lurch uncertainly toward their employment futures.

The role that you play in your business environment makes a big difference in the exit strategy that you will be facing at some point, most likely far in the future.

A good way to determine the tactics that you will need to take in extracting yourself from being owned by The Man is to ask yourself:

Are You a Hunter or a Gatherer?

But please wait and do it on your next break. You are currently being watched by the COO (or maybe it's the CFO), definitely one of the O's.

Take the following simple assessment to help answer this important work related question:

1. When cornered by a frenzied animal or an irate customer do you:
   a. Strike out quickly with a stapler or coffee mug
   b. Dive under a desk
   c. Assign the problem to a worker bee

2. During a business lunch do you order:
   a. The 72 oz. prime rib, blood rare, and eat it with a pocket knife
   b. A small side salad with extra kale and balsamic on the side, with just a sprinkle of Mrs. Dash
   c. A pitcher of the martini special with an olive

3. You see a fellow employee lying unconscious on the sales floor. Do you:
   a. Immediately seek out the victim's attacker, while armed with an out of ink disposable pen
   b. Heat up a can of chicken soup while looking up the number for 911
   c. Tell the victim to get back to work

4. In the office you:
   a. Have a stuffed armadillo on your desk
   b. Have volunteered to be the ficus monitor
   c. Have a large backlit My Way or the Highway sign on your door

5. At the company picnic you:
   a. Build a duck blind out of paper plates
   b. Plant your watermelon seeds for later
   c. Organize a game of Get Back to Work

If you answered (a) for most or all of your answers you are most likely a hunter.

If you answered (b) for most or all of your answers you are most likely a gatherer.

If you answered (c) for most or all of your answers you are most likely a direct descendent of the Chief of the Mean People, currently referred to in most business environments these days as The Boss. Then again you may just have a little gas.

In the real world, every successful business or organization needs a healthy balance of hunters, gatherers, and even bosses to thrive. The Boomers who are still working in any of these roles continue to provide a clear advantage for any organization.

Not only do mature workers have a rich mixture of business and life experience, they also have the benefit of having learned practical and leadership skills via the now long gone apprenticeship and mentoring process that most companies used to utilize.

Of course, you realize that most businesses spawn their bosses from pools of dark green liquid usually kept back by the dumpsters, but that is a story for another day.

You had better get back to hunting or gathering in your old work role. Retirement is still just a gleam in your eye for now. Your new boss has seen you and is waving his arms and pointing in your direction.

However, no need to worry. Having just graduated from junior college, majoring in Instagram Based Selfies, the boss has no idea what you and your team actually do. They tell me his name is Grog.

2

Time Tested Work Strategies

The sun had just risen, pushing away the darkness behind the endless chain of high rise office buildings. Another workday had begun. Coffee was still steaming in the veteran employee's chipped *World's Best Lover* mug that he had found last year in the cafeteria sink on the fourteenth floor.

His cubicle mate was busily plastering a new layer of Hello Kitty images on every available attachable surface of the tiny work area. The aging worker was preparing to hear another round of shouting and swearing, tied to defending the concept that the whiskered icon was an actual cat and not, apparently, someone dressed up like one.

The beleaguered Boomer once again assumed the make myself as small as possible posture and opened a new spreadsheet on the smudged terminal. Another workday had indeed begun.

A stern faced manager approached the cubicle with purpose. "It's Fitzsimmons, right?" he threatened, looking at his quarry with arms folded.

"That's right, sir," responded the wary desk dweller, his real name actually being Smith.

"So, how's that report on the overhead framulators coming? Its due next week you know." The manager's glare intensified.

"Oh, I'm sorry sir," responded the graying worker. "That

project is being handled by young Rutledge over there in cubicle seventy-three. He'll be thrilled that you are thinking about him."

"Of course. I remember now. The guy with the green and purple hair," droned the newly promoted boss while adjusting his tie and toupee. "Now, you keep up the good work there Fitzy. By the way, nice pictures of someone dressed up like a cat."

The harsh reality is that most of you with official Boomer status are still sporting an occupation, and working formally at some level for a boss of some kind. It is also well documented that, at your age, you are usually asleep at your desk, or are about to be.

Truthfully, we know that at this stage in your career the only reason you haven't been let go is that management has forgotten that you still work there at all. Good for you. Just don't mess it up by actually completing any type of task or assignment.

Workplace Tips and Tactics

First, let's briefly discuss the concept of looking busy. Keep your hands held loosely above your keyboard at all times. If you have been texting or watching Charlie's Angels again, be sure to have your *boss key* enabled. Practice exiting your current screen by utilizing a dummy manager intrusion prop. Blowup dolls work best for this, so always keep one nearby.

Another key strategy is to always keep your inbox full to the point of overflowing. It doesn't really matter what you use for this purpose. Old magazines, restaurant takeout menus, and parking tickets work great.

If the rare circumstance occurs of a new task being

somehow put into your inbox, learn to quickly offload it to one of your much younger nearby cubicle companions. This works best if you pick one of the newer employees who has yet to figure out how to do exactly the same thing. In a pinch, lob the assignment onto any random desk on your way out for your next break at the Lady Luck Casino down the street.

One of the more important and beneficial cultural innovations in the last few years is the flex lunch schedule. Properly handled, the astute Boomer can create the illusion that your noon meal time involves uncertain hours between 11:00 AM and 2:30 PM.

Carefully construct a clearly readable desk sign that only includes the words Lunch and Back At printed in bold letters. Add a hand drawn graphic of an analog clock on the sheet. Be sure to include a brad in the middle of the clock face, but leave off the hour and minute hands. Everyone will simply presume that they have just gone missing, and will have no idea when you may or may not return. Enjoy your lunch.

Bathroom breaks are even better. No one has to know that you prefer to use the bathroom in the main bar at the Imperial Hilton on the waterfront. After all, it's your bladder.

Naturally there are many more tactics to be considered to maximize your work experience, including carefully constructed broadcast emails involving a wide variety of family emergencies. Remember that you don't really need to have a cat to have Mr. Fluffy tragically pass away now and then. Be sure to use one of those sad face emoticons in the message.

In fact, by utilizing the tactics described here, some skilled Boomers have reported workdays totaling less than fifteen or twenty minutes a day as an average. Some have actually reported not showing up at all, and still being promoted. You too can make this happen.

Regarding your work skills development, if the worst happens and one of the managers approaches you and mentions starting a new project or a task of some type, quickly use the phrase, "It's about my age, isn't it?" This is the only correct response, and should be embellished by your best stricken face. Once again, practice, practice, practice.

Also, keeping a copy of one of our favorite guidebooks, *Gut 'Em Like a Pig - Age Related Lawsuit Precedents*, conspicuously located on your cubicle bookshelf will be helpful.

As a final important note, these tactics work great for most other types of non-office workplace situations as well. Simply replace the words desk and cubicle with mineshaft or hazardous materials decontamination site, or whatever is appropriate for your field of endeavor.

There you have it! The last few years of your career will zip by as you continue to stare longingly out the window at the retired couples on the street below, who are wearing their matching, brightly colored shirts and sipping margaritas.

We'd be happy to offer further suggestions and recommendations in work avoidance techniques and strategies as well, but it appears that you have dozed off again, and we wouldn't want to wake you.

3

Playing Well with Others

Treadwell was in the lunch room. It wasn't quite time yet for afternoon break, but he'd been taking an extra half hour for lunch each day the last few years. He sat in the corner away from the doorway. Some time ago he discovered that no one actually remembered that he worked for the business at which he had spent his entire career. This made these unscheduled extra breaks safe and simple. He was nearing retirement and if asked, would tell you that he did indeed tire easily these days.

The only other person in the room was the sales manager, still smarting from the unfortunate PowerPoint presentation that indicated another dismal quarter. The downhill graph looked like a ski run. There were reports scattered about the room, having been thrown there by the CEO. The medics were currently giving the beleaguered manager oxygen in the other corner.

Ironically, Treadwell's sales numbers had actually been up for the month. His customer base focused on the quickly expanding needs for the Boomer population, including wineries, casinos, and travel agencies. Soon it would be his turn. He sighed.

On a table in the middle of the room was the last donut from the morning's less than memorable meeting. It was in fact a bear claw. The crispy white glaze that is unique to this particular product outlined the claw indentations perfectly. If there were a prototype for pastries it would surely be this one. The time stamp on the box indicated that it had been baked just a few hours ago.

The sales manager, having somewhat recovered, looked up and noted the prize. This would make up for the meeting's fist fights and threats to his family and pets by the sales staff. Treadwell had been in the room the whole time of course, but as usual, his boss never noticed his presence.

The boss reached for the object of his desire.

Then he noticed the small message written on a sticky note next to the crumb laced container. "Mine," said the note.

The manager looked around once again. A brief unsettled feeling passed through his brain and he hesitated reaching for the delicious morsel. Nothing moved, not a sound. He continued his quest.

Then, moments before he connected with the trophy, he heard a rustling behind the trash can. There was a loud crash and movement from behind, followed by a huge bang. It was the last thing the manager remembered for the remainder of the day.

Treadwell finished his coffee and went back to his desk.

Stan, the lead accounts receivable clerk, slinked away toward the outer offices, donut in hand. He had a deceptively innocent smile on his face as he crunched the pastry. The brass knuckles and truncheon that he had recently purchased from Amazon had been well worth it, he noted.

The clock chimed one-thirty, the perfect time for a claw.

What is an office culture? The concept is not often discussed at any level in the real world of business, but every organization has one. It involves things as big as how you treat your customers and employees, and things as small as how you treat your pastries.

Sometimes there are clues about your specific office culture, such as when various work teams attack other departments with burning brooms and staple pullers. Other times the symptoms are very subtle, including when your co-workers randomly shout, "I REALLY REALLY REALLY HATE THIS PLACE!"

The issues surrounding culture are cross-generational, cross-gender, cross-employee work level, and ironically, cross-cultural. They have become far more complex in the last few years, thanks to the internet. In the workplace everyone can now say literally anything about anyone, whether it is true or not, and complain anonymously about anything and everything pretty much all the time. On rare occasions, some work does still get done, or so they tell me.

Thankfully, most organizations still have a few Boomers working for them. These individuals continue to do some of the actual work. When they all eventually retire, nothing will get done.

For those still working, to help sort out the details of your situation, compare the following examples with your work environment. Of course, there is nothing you can actually do about it at any level from your position, but the details may be fun to share with your therapist.

Signs That Your Corporate Culture May Need Tweaking

- New hire training is three days in the woods with a fish hook and a Snickers bar.

- Your org chart shows 27 VPs managing 25 minions.

- Your key clients refer to your company as Weasel-Tec.

- Business forecasting is contracted out to Madame Zokar's Palms Plus at the mall.

- Your CEO proudly announces that the Every Man for Himself Policy now includes women.

- *We're really sorry* is printed on everyone's business cards.

- The grand prize for your sales promotion is a weaner pig.

- The fire department is called again when an underperforming sales rep actually gets "fired."

- The company mission statement includes the word piranha.

- Performance reviews include the potential of getting voted off the island.

The next time you have the urge to eat a special donut, or hide behind a trash can to catch someone else eating your (so you claim) donut, consider how it relates to your company's corporate culture.

If you like the place at which you work, great! Sadly however, you are the only one left.

If you don't like the place at which you work, we're sorry. Take it up with your department manager after he (yes, in this example it is usually a he) comes out from behind the latest PowerPoint presentation.

In this super competitive marketplace it isn't easy anymore to get ahead in business. This is simply the way it is. Shortly this won't be your problem anymore, will it?

The good news is, thanks to Intel, in a few years your particular position (no, it doesn't matter what your actual job is because we are referring to all of them) will be replaced by a small blinking box that sits on your former desk.

But you won't care. As a retired or laid off Boomer at that point, you'll be in some kind of chair that reclines, somewhere warm, and sipping another drink sporting a tiny umbrella. Maybe later you'll have a bear claw.

And, because the universe has a way of dealing with these things, technology will have advanced by then to the level that the blinking boxes will actually take unauthorized breaks and steal donuts.

Then the laugh will be on them, right?

4

I.T.
The Fist of God

Bank after bank of rotating red lights came on all over the building. Sirens howled hauntingly with that up and down wail that only those who live in the Midwest during a tornado warning can fully describe. Personnel ran back and forth down the halls and between their cubicles. An accounts payable clerk with her cat clutched in her arms, that she had apparently been hiding under her desk for years, ran for the stairwell. "I'll save you, Mittens!" she intoned with purpose.

"We've got a class five breach!" shouted the office manager. "Everybody to your battle stations!"

Beth Smithers had joined the company long before the term "IT" even existed. She had worked her way up through the ranks like they did in the old days, twenty years ago, or so. She had apprenticed in most of the positions on the front line before finally being rewarded with the title of Junior Supervisor after several years of service.

Most of the management staff, at levels far higher than hers, would never have the team leading skills and business acumen that she possessed and invoked every single day behind the scenes. It could even be considered that the company was thriving in general because of her unrewarded practical leadership.

At the moment however, she was busy heading deeper into the building, dodging around the rest of the employees headed for the exits.

Beth was nearing retirement. As a Boomer, the day was drawing closer in which she could hang up her heavy set of door keys forever, but for now, that would have to wait. "Has anyone seen Bill (the CEO)?" she asked, to no one in particular. The sirens continued to wail.

Management had left the building long ago, of course. Most of them were already on the links and through a couple of holes. One of them fleetingly wondered how things were going back at headquarters, but only for a moment. "Where is that beer cart?" questioned the sales manager, missing an easy putt.

Back at the office things had gotten much worse. One of the sales reps sat weeping at his desk, rocking slowly back and forth while intoning, "Why me? Why Me?" All of the other reps had quickly gone missing entirely after looting the cafeteria's gourmet vitamin drink cooler. They felt no fear or remorse because the surveillance cameras were surely not functioning at the moment.

In another part of the building, the accounting department had set up a drum circle along with a fully functional sweat lodge. The bonfire made out of several of the managers' desks seemed out of place. It was a good thing that the fire alarm system was offline as well.

Now it was up to the core team to save the day. The beleaguered Junior Supervisor made her way to the IT department. The door was locked from the inside, as usual. She knocked loudly. Bang! Bang! Bang! "I am invoking section three of the IT handbook," she bellowed. "Open the door immediately!" No response.

"Open the door!" she repeated. "It's a class five breach! THE INTERNET IS DOWN!" No response.

After a few more minutes of silence she heard a distinct

click. The door opened, but just a crack. A scruffy looking, bearded twenty-something millennial, wearing a Grateful Dead t-shirt, Bermuda shorts, and sandals with socks, peered cautiously through the crack. He was eating a cronut.

"Did you turn it off and turn it back on? Is it plugged in?" The door closed again with another loud click.

Now frantic, Smithers raced to the temperature controlled systems room and fumbled with the seven keys needed to open the door. She had received the keys as part of a month long training program and initiation ritual when she first became a manager. The testing sessions had been difficult and daunting, and the bank of forms that she had filled out spanned hundreds of pages. The requirement of actually having to use her own blood to sign the forms seemed a bit much, she had pondered at one point. But eventually she had been given her very own set of keys.

"Now just remember to never ever use them," were the final words spoken by the head of IT at her initiation.

But today was different. An oversized rotating red light flashed in front of her as she stood at the now open doorway to the temperature controlled room containing the mainframe. Other apparently related machines with thousands of small multi-colored lights pulsing along their shining metal fronts lined the walls of the room.

In the corner of the room, behind what appeared to be an espresso machine, was a smallish box labeled Internet Server. Beth approached it cautiously. She inched her way closer to the unit and flicked on the flashlight that she had pulled off one of the unconscious billing department people a couple of floors below.

The light beam splashed against the wall, and ultimately on the back of the machine. She forced herself to look. Before her, snaking away from the server and lying next to an outlet was a gray cord. It was unplugged. Next to the server in a small cardboard box with sides that were too low to effectively contain them, were kittens. "Mew," one of them suggested.

Not long thereafter, the company was back online. The red lights stopped flashing, and after a long wait the sirens stopped. Most of the sales reps who had remained in the building had gone back to surfing porn sites. The other office staff had returned to work as if nothing had happened, and management eventually returned from their meeting at the Bong Bong Club.

Beth Smithers quizzed the now former accounts payable clerk about the unexpected kitten situation, and learned that most of the staff had been using the server room for months, for everything from an apparently successful home brewing operation to raising kittens.

"All you need to do is type in "1234" on the keypad by the door," offered the clerk, as she was cleaning out her desk. Mittens headed for the long existing hole in the wall in the back of the server room, carrying a (computer) mouse in her mouth.

As the soon to be retired Junior Supervisor headed toward the department that she now called The Fist of God, once again to have a little chat, she lamented to herself...*sandy beaches, tall drinks with little umbrellas, blue water, pool boys. Soon. Make it soon.*

5
If Only

The all employees meeting was not going well. Sara, the Regional Director, had just broken up another fight near the overhead projector. The sales staff sat at the back of the room in their generally unsuccessful attempt to escape unnoticed. To make things worse, someone had taken the last piece of Betty's birthday cake.

"I didn't even get one little piece," shouted Betty.

Thankfully, one of the warehouse managers dragged the diminutive office assistant off of the perpetrator before any permanent damage was done, at least by this particular incident.

Sadly, it was the third time this kind of thing had happened in the meeting, as the managers droned on, pointing at pie charts on the screen at the front of the fidgeting assembly.

The presenters continued to high-five each other after another round of off color jokes, apparently unaware of any issues with the conduct of their audience. A stapler whizzed by Sara's left ear.

The seasoned director was not looking forward to the point in the session in which she was going to have to tell the staff that, due to the plummeting sales performance, the sushi and Kobe Beef meat snack machine was going to have a price increase of twenty-five cents per item.

As an apparently hoarded piece of birthday cake flew

past her head and onto the screen at the front of the room, a beleaguered manager ducked behind the podium.

"Sigh," she muttered to herself. "I think it may be time to consider my options."

Eventually the day will come when you entertain the humorous concept that you can retire at some point in the distant future. The word has many different meanings, of course, depending on things such as your personality type, your family culture, and, let's see, do you have any money?

For discussion purposes only, let's assume you have actually saved enough funds so that, along with your meager social security check, you can contemplate retirement. They do say that fantasizing is good for your brain.

Now we know that you have already read the thousands of pre-retirement articles in the money or business sections of your favorite website. They have wonderful topics like "Ten Best Retirement Places to Dock Your Yacht" and "Seven Ways to Become a Successful Central American Retiree via the Lucrative Drug Mule Trade."

The list of pundits advising you when, if, and how you should retire is long indeed. There are also some great formulas to calculate your ability to afford it. There is the *four percent rule* discussion, the *Is a million enough?* contemplation, and of course, the trick question, *When should I take my social security?*

While that is all well and good, here is how your progression to a potential retirement is really going to play out for you in ten easy steps:

1. Your boss yells at you again for leaving out a comma on page three in your report, and you say to yourself again, *I really need to get the hell out of here.* And this time you really mean it.

2. You talk with your significant other about it, and suggest that she keep working while you retire. Much later, after the divorce, the doctors advise you that you may recover some of the feeling in your torso and back with time.

3. You commit to and complete the due diligence on all of your finances, investments, assets, and savings. After several impressive spreadsheets are developed, with headings and colored borders, the available funds add up to twelve dollars.

4. You contact the Social Security Administration and get a complete printout of the various scenarios for starting your withdrawals. Ironically, the best case option shows an average dispersal of twelve dollars. At least it's per month.

5. You review your company retirement plan. It turns out that you apparently forgot to fill out the paperwork a few years back. However, you did achieve the marginal attendance bonus which would produce a one-time payout at retirement of twelve dollars.

6. You call your parents at their summer retreat in the Bahamas. In Spanish, the individual answering the phone advises you that they moved a few months ago without a forwarding address.

7. You buy fifty dollars worth of lottery tickets and win...twelve dollars.

8. You request and are granted a meeting with your boss to discuss a possible sizable severance package if you were to leave the company due to stress.

9. You are immediately dismissed from the organization and escorted out of the building.

10. You go online and look up jobs on Craig's List, apply for and get a new gig in Central America. You buy a one way ticket to Guadalajara. In passing, you wonder what a drug mule actually does.

Finally, you realize and admit that retirement will have to wait for a while. You look one last time in your wallet and discover, well, you know.

Meanwhile, the bus with you aboard continues relentlessly South in the night.

Part 2

Transition and Transformation

6

Last Day

"Hey Seth, got a minute?" coaxed the department manager. Seth of course, was a bit concerned that he may have left the coffee pot on overnight in the executive lunchroom and burned down the fourth floor again. But he had little choice, and proceeded down the hall to the corner office.

"So, how long have you been here, umm, buddy?" queried the thirty year old executive manager.

"Well let me think," pondered Seth. "When was Harry Truman president?"

"It really doesn't matter," said the boss. "The committee thinks that it is time for you to consider retiring. What are your thoughts about that?"

"Retiring?" considered Seth.

"Good choice," interrupted the manager. "Please have your desk cleared out by noon today. We'll be having a five minute ceremony for you in the parking garage. Betty said she'll bring down a few cupcakes from the former lunchroom. And thanks for your years of service. See you buddy...got a racket ball match in ten minutes." Seth looked up to see his former boss heading quickly down the hall and around the corner.

He walked into the hallway and shuffled back to his desk of many years. He noticed that his fake rubber tree had died again, and that his *World's Second Best Dad* coffee mug had another chip in it. Finally he packed his few possessions into a donut box and slowly headed down to the garage. It was noon.

Whether through planning, circumstances, old age, or more probably death, eventually you will retire. To be completely honest, if you are dead we probably can't help you. However, the rest of you will absolutely need some guidance as you wind your way through the morass of things you will need to do to finally graze contentedly in the fertile pasture of your future. We, of course, are here to help.

The day you finally decide to pull the corporate plug, all manner of thoughts will race through your head. *What was I thinking?* usually comes first, followed quickly by, *No, really, what the heck was I thinking?*

Not unlike the five stages of grieving, you will ultimately embrace acceptance and begin the practical process of heading into your official retirement.

The gate to the pasture will finally open and you will, with the appropriate amount of trepidation, walk through and close it slowly behind you.

Here are a few key things that you must do on the day of your transition:

- Reassure those around you that you have some money. It will throw off your family and friends, at least for a while.

- Tell your significant other that you are retiring. You would have had to do this eventually at some point anyway.

- Confirm with your boss and company that you are retiring. This will be easy because they already thought that you actually retired some years ago.

- Clean out your desk. Remove all emails that involve your ongoing harmless, playful interchange with the administrative assistant on the fourth floor, and delete all of your adult internet sites that you signed up for with your manager's MasterCard.

- Go to your retirement party if your company unexpectedly chooses to give you one. You can always use one more fake gold watch or related ten dollar trinket, and there might be cake.

- Leave the building with your cardboard box of staplers and your dead rubber tree plant. Find a bar, and drink heavily until someone eventually discovers where you are and drives you home.

Welcome to what many have begun calling your new work. At first you may have some minor disorientation in regards to actually being retired. For the first few weeks you will get up every morning and catch the bus into town. Your family will call 911 every time they see you in the kitchen during daylight hours, and your dog will hide under the house.

Many new retirees have solved this issue by hiding the number for 911, and proactively moving under the house with the dog for the first few months, although the dog probably won't like it.

Sometime much later, you may find the courage to uncurl from the fetal position and climb out from the crawl space. Much later than that, your family will begin to recognize you in the daylight, and you will have begun taking in small amounts of food again.

In many early stage retirement cases, the spouse will

have forgotten completely about you, with your living under the house and all, and will have remarried. Some retirees actually consider this a plus.

In any case, first clean yourself up a bit. Use soap. Then coax the dog out, reintroduce yourself to your family, and most importantly, find where you left your smart phone and give it a name. I named mine Ficus. We'll talk more about this later.

This completes stage one of the Pasture Process. You are now officially retired. Pour yourself one of those fancy drinks with an umbrella and a name that you can't say in front of the kids, and sit back in your vibrating recliner.

Congratulations buddy!

7

Re-Emergence

Now What?

There was another flare-up in the kitchen. The chef threw up his arms in disgust at yet another failed soufflé. "You miserable people can't ever get anything right, can you?" he shouted to his staff, meaning wife and children in this case, who were cowering under the stove again.

His chef hat was askew and in danger of catching fully on fire. But he just didn't care. The soufflé had to be perfect.

This great chef, or master grilling sensei, as he liked to call himself these days, had been retired from his previous career as a tax accountant for over a month now.

Until today the great chef had never cooked anything in his life except some poorly boiled water in 1986. The family was understandably anxious for him to settle into his life of retirement.

Yesterday he had been talking about his next big plan to repair motorcycles, or maybe start up his own taxidermy business. Surely either one of those would be better than any of his previous plans.

Another pan flew through the air towards the refrigerator.

As you might well expect, there are several steps to evolving into your new retirement paradigm. Many recent participants have compared the process to herding cats, only far more complex and difficult.

A few of the basic evolutionary steps include:

- Burning all of your work suits or dresses and all related work paraphernalia, including the dozen staplers and the copy machine that you borrowed on your last day. Ties are to get special emphasis via the paper shredder, which you also borrowed. However, keep one tie for your next funeral.

- Embracing wine and beer as a food group.

- Having the epiphany that you can be of great help around the house in all sorts of ways.

- Accepting the restraining order to stay fifty yards from your house, established by your spouse or significant other, and their team of lawyers.

- Noticing for the first time that there is a casino only six hours away on the Indian Reservation.

- Realizing one day that you don't have to get up at 6:30 AM any more. Since most alarm clocks are very difficult to reprogram, consider other means to change the settings. In our experience, larger hammers work better.

- Becoming a regular at the local Starbuck's, where they have begun shouting "Norm" to you every time you stop by. You learn the birthdays, relationship situations, and many other intimate details about all of the current and former employees. And you now know how to make a double nonfat caramel latte.

- Accepting the restraining order requiring you to stay at least fifty feet away from the local Starbuck's.

- Starting to look for the coin collection that you had as a kid, with the certainty that there will be a rare issue somewhere in the shoe box that will stabilize your retirement. Your soon to be former significant other will remind you that have already used all the coins to buy lattes at the local Starbuck's.

- Deciding to mow your lawn every day, even in the middle of winter, and to name all of the azaleas and rose bushes. Bubba and Miss Kitty are your current favorites.

Then one morning you awaken to the smell of bacon cooking and coffee brewing in the kitchen, while your mate whistles Clementine in the background.

You will pause, and finally think to yourself, *retirement isn't really so bad I suppose. I really need to get on with things.*

Then you will step on a broken piece of the alarm clock, requiring several stitches. But that's okay. Your new work beckons. Let's begin.

8

Downsizing

Your New Home

The golf cart hurtled down the hallway. We were out of pickles again in the kitchen and I had received the assignment of retrieving some from the storage room at the east end of the house. I had actually been there once before a few years back. *Let's see, turn left at the atrium, I think. No, that didn't work.*

Eventually I called my support team on the cell phone and got directions, and a few short hours later arrived at the storage room. Sadly, there were no pickles to be found. I made my way back to the west end of the house where the family was waiting for their expected condiment.

"No pickles," I announced.

"Did you look behind the balsamic vinegar near the pallet of baked beans?" quizzed my spouse.

On my way back to the storage room, after I missed the turn again and ended up in the pool area, I considered the concept of downsizing. Maybe a five thousand square foot house was not really necessary now that there were just the three of us, which included our currently missing cat Fur Ball Two.

We had bought the house back before the prices skyrocketed, when we succumbed to the upward mobility status model that everyone else at work was doing during that time. They used to call houses like ours McMansions.

The good news is that the house filled the entire lot, from setback to setback, leaving the tiniest of yards. It made mowing easy, particularly since I recently acquired the Acre Master-3000 farm ready riding tractor, which now took up our entire three bay garage.

A few years after our home purchase, the local politicians caught wind of the great potential of houses like ours as a vehicle for producing some significant revenues for their many critical taxing needs, such as having a special election to pick the town's favorite donut.

As marginally retired Boomers, living in a huge house did not make sense for us any longer, as we moved relentlessly forward into our new work and the pasture beyond.

However, as we considered downsizing, there was still the minor issue that one or more of our soon to be middle-aged kids would be moving back in again in the near future.

In fact, just last week a couple of the kids actually did return home, or so I have been told. I do remember that one of them had appeared briefly in the entertainment lounge yesterday. The middle kid, I believe. There were a couple of much younger people in the house, too. These may have been some of our grandkids. I'll have to check.

It was time to sell the house. Of course the irony was that, although we had purchased a huge home, we only had about fifty dollars equity in it as the day to sell it arrived. Naturally, we could have made a wonderful profit a few years back. But the market plummeted the day before we decided to go for it and take our profit, and has never recovered since. In fact, we have been told that when we sell the house, we will actually owe the realtor money for the commission. However, they say that we can keep the signing pen.

In the meantime, the taxes on the property and the utilities skyrocketed. Last year they added a *just in case we can think of something in the future to spend it on* tax.

It was time to move to a more reasonable housing and lifestyle situation at last.

We had been reading about what the experts are calling minimalism. It sounded great, and I was ready to become a card carrying disciple of the program. Shortly after our latest tax audit and subsequent garnishments, we proudly decided that it was officially time to downsize.

Here are a few things to help you downsize the right way:

Keys to Successful Downsizing

- Forget thinking about the square footage of your home. Instead consider how easy your *unit* is to move to another campground.

- Who needs a formal bathroom anyway? There is plumbing in the kitchen.

- Don't use any Winnebago or related motor home floor plans as a model. They are much too large.

- You might consider a condo, but that would involve neighbors.

- When your kids come to visit they can always pitch a tent.

- To save money, think about one of the smaller, burned out homes right at the end of the local international airport's runway.

- Furniture is really overrated. Keep two webbed patio chairs, a cardboard box for an end table, and a blowup mattress. That will be more than plenty. However, be sure to keep the ninety inch flat screen TV.

- Before moving in, make sure your new home has a roof. We looked at several being offered without one, and they were indeed less expensive, but we ultimately vetoed the idea when a bird started building a nest in the realtor's hair.

Ultimately we chose a home with around fifteen hundred square feet in a modest neighborhood and it is working out just fine.

We got a great deal on the property because there is a slaughterhouse and rendering plant at the end of the block. It is really not a problem, although my eyes do burn a bit when the wind is from the south, and our dog has gone missing.

9

Downsizing

Your New Roof

In the early years of humankind, getting work done was somewhat simpler than it is today. Depending on your size, you either threatened someone with a giant club or Pterodactyl bone, or someone threatened you with one. One way or the other the work got done. Then the waffle iron was invented and things got a bit more complicated.

Let's say you finally have to put a new roof on your house. The rain is coming into your kitchen onto the stove, and you can't make omelets puff up correctly anymore. To make it even worse, you have recklessly decided to live in a big, soulless, cosmopolitan city.

There is hope however, for the alert Boomer, because we are here to help.

As a starting point, below are listed a few of the several hundred steps in the process that you will certainly encounter:

- Friends form a committee to tell you that you need a new roof. Your excuses about your indoor swimming pool and having stock in the tarp business just don't cut it anymore.

- In a breakthrough with your therapist, you agree to do it.

- You ask your friends if they know a good roofer. They don't.

- You go online and Google *new roof*, and thousands of ads for hair restoration pop up immediately, most of them pornographic. You consider, hesitate, and then move on.

- You finally find a local roofing contractor and make the call. No one answers, so you leave a message. Three days later a woman with a strong accent actually calls you back. She informs you that their headquarters is located in New Jersey, and that someone would be happy to stop by in November as part of their annual national tour. You decline the offer.

- Finally an office colleague remembers that he used to know someone who had a friend whose cousin's brother-in-law was a roofer. He advises you that for only fifteen hundred dollars he will give you the number. Of course, you immediately pay the finder's fee and make the call.

- A disembodied voice answers the phone. "Press one for toilets, two for our online casino, three for IT support, and four for roofing," announces a pre-recorded message with an accent.

- You inadvertently press three. Someone asks if you unplugged it and plugged it back in. You press four.

- A mechanical voice springs to life. "Need a new roof?" it intones. *"The 900 Easy Steps to Hiring a Roofing Contractor* is now available at an affordable price. Just mail your enrollment fee of two thousand dollars to our processing center in Romania. Then let the fun begin!" Reluctantly, you place the order.

Then again, if you happen to live in a small city or town

as we do, the process unfolds somewhat differently. It goes like this:

- You need a new roof.

- While waiting at a stop light one morning, you write down the number of one of the several dozen local roofing contractors who has a nice looking van.

- You call the number. Bill answers. He meets you at your house later that morning.

- You agree to a price. Bill notes it on a used cocktail napkin that he has in his van, and you shake hands.

- Later that week, Bill shows up at your house with fifteen or so workers and the materials needed to roof your house.

- They roof your house.

- You pay the bill to Bill with cash. Many of the workers invite you to their homes for dinner.

- You wave as they drive away and contemplate your next project...maybe a catfish pond.

In the real world, there you sit waiting, floating in the living room of your big city home. The rain beats down on your head, and your smart phone has just disappeared under the waves. You could always go out and find a Pterodactyl bone, I suppose.

Or you could move here. If you do, stop on by our place and stay a while. We'll have a fish boil.

10

Downsizing

Your New Water Heater

In the realm of explosions throughout time, the one that was now producing an impressive mushroom cloud rising into the sky wasn't really that big. We had seen even larger ones before in various parts of our own neighborhood and small town. Then again, as the fire trucks were pulling away, we decided to designate this one as at least an *eight* on our evolving blast scale.

It was a Sunday night of course. The clock read 2:59 AM. We had just discovered that the pilot light had gone out on the gas water heater again, the third time this month.

"No problem," I posed, gathering the necessary tools from their prominent spot in our laundry room.

Shortly thereafter, sirens screamed as all manner of response equipment emerged from their staging sites, and headed to our house. Dogs howled in support. It was no coincidence that the local fire department had recently awarded us customer of the month, and that the precinct was named in our honor.

In our defense, the gas water heater was already installed when we bought the house. We had studied a bit about the pros and cons of electric versus gas when shopping for a new home. Our conclusion was that electric furnaces and water heaters cost slightly more than the gas versions to operate. So naturally we immediately vetoed the electric option completely.

"You know why they make you put water heaters up eighteen inches from the floor?" posed the inspector who was digging through the rubble. "It is so the explosion won't be quite so big when the gas leaks out of your lawnmower in the garage, exposing the fumes to the pilot light," he finished. "Too bad yours wasn't set up like that."

Shortly thereafter, while looking for our next new home, the nice real estate agent advised us that this particular house did indeed have a natural gas water heater, and even disclosed that the pilot light was currently not working. But then he said that this exact brand of heater was easy to get restarted, and that they hardly ever blow up, or so he had heard. So no problem.

Later that day we signed the papers, and later that month we moved in. Now to restart the heater:

Restarting the Pilot Light on your Gas Water Heater

- Call the fire department now. Why wait?

- Assemble the tools needed:
    - Jaws-of-Life (2 sets - deluxe jaw model)
    - Fire retardant
    - NASA approved protective suit with visor hood and mittens
    - Screw driver assortment (see sizing manual, pages 19-210)

- Monkey wrenches, sizes extra-large through humongous
- Tweezers
- A light source of some kind (optional)
- Matches

- Initiate the pilot light restart process (see below).

- Find the valve that connects the main gas line to the water heater. These usually can be found under the house near or below the sewage drain. Often the valve is buried, and must be dug out with a pick and shovel. Take care not to puncture the gas line or the sewage drain at this point. Turn off the gas line valve before starting, if you can find it.

- Return to the water heater and put on the fire retardant suit. In most cases this should take no more than two hours to complete. Note: experienced technicians recommend using the bathroom *before* starting this step.

- Locate the water heater's internal primary disrupter assembly housed on the underside and back of your unit (see diagram 975A). Note the obstructing wire bundle array and the double thick protective access plates that were installed and sealed at the factory, that are covering the pilot light assembly. These will need to be removed to access the pilot light valve.

- Position the Jaws-of-Life carefully around the water heater and activate. Note that the second set is recommended to have on hand simply as a precaution in the event that you cannot get the first set to release after use. This will expose the pilot light sector.

- Remove the screws (420 each) from the frame. It is important to understand that each screw is configured with a different type of thread and head size. Some of the screws also require a reverse removal technique (see page 1094 part 12). Be careful to avoid the temperature sensing array obstructing this unit. Failure to do so will result in catastrophic consequences (see catastrophic consequences, chapter 19).

- Grasp the pilot light housing firmly with the monkey wrench and tweezers. Gently twist counterclockwise at a forty-five degree angle. Note that any deviation from this process will void the warranty, and will of course break off the housing connections, allowing any captured gas in the line to escape into the room and ignite. Expose the valve.

- Locate the unit control matrix on the front of the water heater (see diagram alley). There are six color-coded buttons that must be depressed in a specific timed sequence. Practice this process carefully before actually attempting (see catastrophic consequences, chapter 19).

- Turn the gas line valve on again under your house.

- At the front of the water heater begin depressing the buttons in the correct order. With your other hand, light the pilot light assembly at the back of the unit with the match.

- Count to one thousand.

- At this point the pilot light should ignite. If it doesn't, repeat all of the steps above.

- Replace the screws on the protective frame in reverse order, and finally replace the protective plate.

That's all there is to it!

Shopping for and installing your water heater

After twenty years or so, your current water heater with its six year warrantee will need to be replaced. In fact, we have known people who have had to trade in their units after only fifteen years, just because the water started pooling in their kitchen, basement, and attic.

To make the proper purchasing decision you will need to do your due diligence on the best specifications for your family's water heating needs. First answer these important questions:

1. Do you have ten or more children and/or pets?

2. Do you live by a large nuclear facility or electrical substation?

3. What year were you born?

4. Do you sometimes need to use the restroom more frequently than you think you should?

5. Do you know the difference between an abrasion and a contusion?

6. And most importantly, do you own stock in Noxious Natural Gas, or one of its regional units?

If you answered yes to one or more of these inquiries, you are an ideal candidate for focusing on a natural gas water heater as your best option.

FAQ's

What size water heater do I need?

Most families select one of the standard 30, 40, or 50 gallon versions. However, have you ever wanted to take another twenty minute shower and run out of hot water? This is exactly why we recommend the 4500 gallon XTremeMegaFlo industrial unit with hyper-gas-input jetting as the best option. After all, if these heaters can supply the needs of a two thousand employee high rise, then it should work fine for you.

Where should I buy?

Online of course. However, the recommended unit won't fit in a standard forty foot semi truck, so there may be a bit of an added freight charge to consider. And, at this point only China can (is willing to) supply the XTMF because it does not meet any of the environmental laws of the United States. So there may be a bit of an upcharge due to shipping your unit through the Canary Islands.

How much should I pay?

This is a natural question (ha ha), and we are happy to help. Let's just say that once you've decided to acquire the XTMF, the sellers will find a way for you to afford it. You may be asked at some future date to handle a favor or two, but that is nothing for you to worry about right now.

Can I still get home owners insurance if I own the XTMF?

No

What about the Installation?

Generally, we would recommend that you hire professionals to install your unit. After all, it is a highly complex and intricate piece of equipment. However, as an experienced water heater owner you may choose to go it alone. There is a 12,000 page instruction manual included in your purchase, and some of it is in what is described as English. You'll need a screwdriver.

It has been several days now since our new natural gas water heater, that we bought to replace the one that lost its pilot light and subsequently marginally exploded, arrived. We opted to buy a more conventional brand from Home Depot that only cost about $1000, and of course decided to install it ourselves.

We are still just a bit concerned that, during the installation, I may have cross-threaded one of the 420 mounting crews...or maybe not.

Good luck with your decision to acquire a new natural

gas water heater. We sometimes still toy with the idea that it was worth the risk.

If all else fails you could always buy an electric one.

11

Pest Control

Regarding Bats

It's three AM and blissful, revitalizing REM sleep has overtaken us. The dreams, ah the dreams. And then it begins. Scritch, scritch, scritch. Pause. Scritch, scritch, scratch. Repeat. It goes on endlessly for the next several hours, again.

But this night is different. There is a bang, another bang, and suddenly a wild flapping of wings around our heads. Out into the hallway it careens, clearly looking for something. A way out, I surmise, and rush downstairs to fling open the front door. It pauses, looks at me with contempt and flies out into the night. You see, bats are smart. I read it in a book.

Documentaries and articles about bats abound on the internet and television these days. Since The Incident I have in fact learned a great deal about them.

During my research I happened upon *Bats are our Buddies - Part 12* on satellite channel 937, the Winged Pest and Rodent Channel. It was an epiphany of sorts for me because I finally made peace with the reality that we had bats in our attic, and that they had to go away - far, far away.

It seemed so simple at first. Find the hole. Plug the hole. Done. As it turns out there are a few more steps, but more about this later.

They always start the television programming involving bats with millions of them heading out from under the bridge in Austin, Texas every evening towards Mexico, just as the sun sets. I am convinced it is the bat army's way of avoiding taxes and accessing affordable healthcare, but that is just a theory.

It is quite an enjoyable scene, I understand, except for the few tourists lost each day who have inadvertently wandered into the bats' flight path at launch time. Not a bad cost really, considering the spectacle's advertising value for the city.

As it turns out, bats are endangered in many areas. Teams of scientists have been dispatched to discover why this is happening. Is it the climate? Predators? Diet? Politics? No one is really sure.

They could have just called me, of course. Think about it. When was the last time you heard about any belfries being built? No belfries, no bats. It's that simple.

The poor creatures have tried to substitute for their natural instincts by nesting in belfry-like alternatives such as caves, restaurants, and of course, my attic. Sadly, their population continues to dwindle.

The obvious solution is to provide tax incentives for individuals and corporations seeking to pursue the lucrative belfry and attic market. It seems like they should have thought of this long ago.

Critical Things to know about Bats

- If they bite you, you will die.

- If they don't bite you but fly around your house for a while and then exit through your front door, you will still need to get the painful series of two hundred rabies shots. Then you will die.

- There are two basic sizes of bats, big and huge.

- Bats are the only animals whose babies are not cute.

- They hang upside down just to piss everyone off.

- When you see one bat you can be sure there are several thousand more lurking nearby, usually in your closet.

- Bats are nocturnal, and they want to be sure you know it.

- Batman doesn't really look anything like the bats that I have seen. Real bats are much bigger.

- Bats are actually mammals, not birds. The bird phylum didn't want to have anything to do with them.

- The only things in the world worse than bats are mosquitoes, which bats eat. Ironic, eh?

- Bonus bat fact: Guano: it's more than a pretty name.

It turns out that there are actually several hundred steps to removing bats from an attic. Ultimately, we surrendered and called The Bat Guy. He and his team showed up in a truck that looked like a Hummer, only much larger. He was great. And after learning terms like eliminators, big honking holes, and never seen nothing like that before, we hired the team.

The thousands of dollars we put down as a starting point

were well worth it. It's been a few months now and they tell us it won't be much longer before they can actually start the process of removing the bats.

As we learned, you can't actually remove the bats from your attic during most of the year. In the winter they are hibernating, and if you plugged up all of the escape holes they would eventually have to learn to eat insulation. That would be very bad (see endangered above).

In the spring, fall, and summer you can't remove the bats either. The experts tell us that they have to want to come out on their own accord. Consequently, we have been advised that someday, when the moment is right, they will actually install the previously mentioned eliminators.

These high-tech devices allow the bats to get out of your attic through a tube, but then they can't get back in because the tube is too small in one direction (or something like that). Sweet.

The only small issue is that this process takes several years to complete before the new team of bat removal workers (the original ones will have long since retired) seal up the openings for good. We wouldn't want any of the slower bug eaters to wake up and be stuck...because then they would die.

The next time you are out in the yard late in the evening and feel a whoosh of wind, hear a frantic cheeping sound, and experience the unmistakable pinch of a bite on the back of your neck, please remember that bats are our friends. They are endangered through no fault of their own. And once again, they eat bugs.

If you are bitten, they say that most bats possibly don't have rabies anyway. You'll be fine.

12

Pest Control

Ants Go Marching

The tunnel seemed to be endless and it was very dark indeed. Forager #379625B or Bubba, as his closest friends called him, had been traveling for some time now through the mysterious passage. He hadn't been all that successful lately. That incident in which he tried to drag a full six pack of Budweiser back to the nest by himself did not turn out well. It was time for some good news.

Suddenly far ahead in the distance a dim light appeared. It was getting brighter with every step. The passageway narrowed dramatically at this point and Bubba almost decided to turn back. But then a small fragment of wood chipped away and he was through. *I think they call this a kitchen,* he contemplated.

He was overcome for a bit and just huddled in the opening, but upon seeing the vast riches in every direction he decided to venture out into the new world he had found. *I think I'll name it Xanadu,* he decided.

He would be famous. Maybe now Betty Anne would finally agree to stop calling him gross and go out on that date he imagined. He even thought he might be smelling bacon. It was perfect.

The intrepid forager knew that his next mission was to head back to the nest while leaving the all important pheromone trail for the rest of the brigade (Unit 9241-West) to follow. But what would be the harm in just a bite or two of what appeared to be a fully intact Skittle that was clearly no more than a few inches ahead, and just sitting on a large flat surface. In fact it appeared to be - yes - lemon!

After impatiently waiting for several minutes as he had been taught in his advanced foraging class, he decided that there was no danger at all. Then he chuckled to himself as he remembered the joke his teacher shared with him in the hall after test finals were turned in. What do they call the student with the lowest grade in foraging class? A forager, right?

He climbed out of the tunnel sporting a broad grin and a swagger, and headed purposely toward the waiting treat.

He was nearly at his destination, his magnificent prize gleaming just ahead. Time to eat!

Then however, he sensed...something. The sky darkened. He looked up, antennae waving to get a better idea of the intruder. His last thoughts were of the fresh smelling facial tissue that had come out of nowhere to snatch him away from his prize and his destiny.

As he faded, he believed he saw a monstrous form hovering over him and heard, from a place far away, "Hey look, a Skittle - five second rule. Eewww! An ant!"

Then everything went black.

Important Things You Should Know About Ants

- If ants were the size of humans they would be much bigger.

- They can lift many times their weight, but usually find someone else to do it for them.

- If you see a few ants you can be sure there are thousands more back in the nest, often watching football.

- In the real world ants do not go marching one by one. In fact, those who attempt it are fined by the union.

- There is no direct evidence that Terminex was actually started by a group of militant red ants trying to take control of Topeka, although TMZ claims it has pictures.

- Ants do indeed like to move rubber trees. It apparently is a pride issue.

- Poison of any strength is useless against ants, although it has been shown to give some of them a slight rash.

- There are no ants in Antarctica, or antelopes either, for that matter.

Have Ants? We Can Help.

We recently were the victims of a major ant infestation in our home. One day everything was just fine, and the next there were parades of ants going in and out of almost every room in the house. It looked a lot like Mardi Gras, but without the beads.

Our friends told us that since they were just little black ants we had nothing to worry about. They said that ants don't eat very much, and they don't even bite unless provoked.

Mistake One

The ants had to go, of course. We called several exterminators for an estimate. The first question each of the local ant guys asked when we called was, "So who is your favorite mortgage broker?" We ultimately decided to go it alone.

Mistake Two

My wife is a part time environmentalist and suggested that we find a way to rid ourselves of the ants in an environmental and humanitarian method. The main internet solution for this was to simply mix some borax with jelly, wait a few days for the borax to humanely kill off the entire nest, and then go on with your life. We put out dozens of traps.

Mistake Three

After a week or two we determined that the homemade traps weren't completely successful. In fact, it appeared that, through incomplete merging of the borax and jelly we had inadvertently enlarged the ant colony more than a hundredfold.

We agreed to abandon the supposed humane approach and bought some commercial ant traps. Upon reflection it would have made sense to read the labels before we placed several hundred traps throughout the house (costing just under $1295). As it turns out, the main active ingredient in the traps we purchased was...borax.

Mistake Four

We then opted to use the more direct approach and bought a few gallons of extra strength ant spray at the local hardware store. Once again we should probably have read the label. Although the ants continued to thrive after our extensive application of the product, our entire family was subsequently hospitalized for a few weeks.

The doctors have advised that some of us will recover the use of one or more of our limbs eventually, although the hearing and tooth loss will unfortunately be permanent.

Mistake Five

Then we went out and bought an anteater. Thank goodness for Craig's List. The friendly entrepreneur we met up with in a back alley was confident that it would do the trick and quickly rid us of our infestation.

He said the anteater's name was Brad. Unfortunately Brad died after a few days. After tracking the previous owner to a local prison cell, the seller advised us that Brad was probably allergic to the particular kind of ants in our house, or possibly borax, and that the no return policy would still apply. Go figure.

And now we apparently are featured on PETA posters throughout the area.

Mistake Six

By this time the use of fire was making complete sense. We had been told that ants really don't like fire and would probably move out if it was prevalent near their nest.

Mistake Seven

We really did believe that our home owner's insurance would cover the loss of our home due to fire. They now tell us that, while generally true, if you burn the house down yourself they won't cover your loss.

The Solution

Our new home is just great. We have been living here a few months and have yet to see an ant. Of course, it is still winter.

The Future

Since we had so much difficulty ridding ourselves of the ants, we figured that if you can't beat them, join them. Consequently, we have just invested in our first ant farm.

Our real estate broker working out of the projects has assured us that the swamp land we have purchased will be an ideal site to start the farm. And luckily his brother happens to be in the ant food business. He gave us a great discount on our first truckload of Purina Ant Chow.

The contractors who will be building the required barns and stables are scheduled to begin work on Monday.

Hopefully, you will find this input helpful if you ever encounter a persistent ant problem. Forget those pricey pros, we say. Like us, you can now go out there and *make some lemons out of lemonade.*

13

Pest Control

Relatives

Water cascaded down the mountainside near the cave. The winter snow was finally beginning to melt, and the first hints of spring could be seen as a green tinge to the meadows and forest floor of this remote location.

The intrepid hunter was returning from a very successful mission. His creel was full of fat trout captured easily from the quickly flowing river that ran a mile or so beyond the hidden home site. The hunter's mate was also nearing the cave entrance with a large basket full of select mushrooms and greens from the nearby wooded wonderland. It was going to be another good day. Life in their wilderness retreat continued to be great in every way.

In fact, the only incident to mar their life in paradise was an unexpected visit by a mother bear a couple of weeks back, in which they lost a side of beef out of their well-stocked larder.

Their home was hundreds of miles from the nearest town, or civilization of any kind for that matter. Jet plane trails could be seen high overhead, but that couldn't be helped.

The Boomer couple had moved here a few months ago after things had gotten unexpectedly out of hand at their previous home near the city.

Before the move to the wilderness in Central Montana,

the pair had recently retired to the suburbs after a lifetime in the workplace. They were settling in nicely to their new lifestyle when the visits began.

"Hi Mom. Hi Dad. Anybody home?" chimed one of their young adult daughters, who had entered the front door with a key that had come from somewhere.

"I won't be a minute. Just stopped by to get a couple of things out of the fridge. With the kids and all, I forgot to stop by the grocery store again. Are you going to be using that side of beef or that home baked apple pie for anything? I'll just take them. Okay? Byeee."

And the visits continued. Their other daughter and son independently decided to move back home with their spouses and children a few nights later. That situation in itself would not have been so bad, but there never seemed to be any hot water.

Then the aunt and uncle from Minnesota, whom they had never met, showed up at the door one day. A full sized Winnebago was parked in the driveway and half way out into the street, completely blocking the garage, which still held the family car.

"Hello? Anybody home?" filtered in from the porch. "Hope you guys don't mind. We are on our way to Las Vegas again and just thought we would drop by to visit for a few weeks. Sure glad you guys are retired now. We used our key to get in, okay? Say, you're not going to use that full side of beef in the fridge, are you?"

The visits continued. And requests for favors poured in from every direction, all beginning with the phrase, *Since you're retired now...*

There was the "Would you mind dropping the kids off at

hip-hop class?" The "Would you hang out with the kids while I go to bar tending school?" And the "Please pick up another side of beef at the farm. We'll pay you back later" requests. In all cases the word request was used ironically.

Then things began to escalate. There were the "Would you be willing to co-sign for our new yacht?" style inquiries. And of course the expected "Your cousin Shank is in jail again. Tag. You're it. Your turn to bail him out, buddy."

That was the last straw.

The couple moved out in the night. It was raining and the relatives were all asleep. There was a light on in the bathroom of the Winnebago, which was understandable since Uncle Phil had irreparably clogged the toilet in the house again. And since the motor home was blocking the door they had to cut a hole in the side of the garage to move the car, but in the end it was well worth the effort.

All was quiet as they pulled away, looking back at their former home for the last time. Later they heard that no one actually knew they were gone for several weeks. It turns out that at some point one of the relatives was in the mood for some beef and couldn't find any in the fridge.

Life was indeed wonderful at the well hidden mountain retreat - until one day they heard the bushes moving outside the cave entrance.

"Hello? Anybody home? It's Uncle Phil."

Relatives have a critical role in the success of the Boomer retirement model. They can be amazingly supportive and helpful during the often difficult transition from being fully employed to a time in which boredom and loneliness are often lurking. However, they can also cause some issues.

Here are a few pointers to help you maximize your relative experience during retirement:

- Tell your children that you have moved to Guatemala.

- Move to Guatemala.

- If you can't move, black-out curtains and a locking garage are a must.

- Never have a spare front door key hidden anywhere.

- Plant trees and shrubs in any area that may allow a Winnebago to be parked.

- Learn to breathe quietly when someone is at the front door. If you have pets, buy a muzzle.

- Lock your refrigerator and never buy a side of beef.

- One day in the middle of the night, drive your car to a trailhead somewhere, park it and start walking.

Someday there will likely be colonization of the planet Mars. For those Boomers still in the pre-retirement phase of their new work evolution, it may actually be possible to buy a ticket at some point.

Of course, if this does occur, presumably your relatives will be able to travel there as well. Your best bet will be to hide away in one of the many mountain ranges after you get there. We have heard that the Martians there are very friendly and know how to play bridge. It is also well known that Martians do not eat beef.

The best part of all is that Martian children begin working in their teens and proactively move out to begin supporting their parents after they have finished school.

And apparently they don't have uncles.

14

The New Millennium

Technology's Bitch

It happened again just this morning. As retired Boomers, we sat down to breakfast with our laptops carefully angled on the table to allow room for the food. Today was one of those days in which the screen announced the need to reboot.

Various operating system updates had apparently been launched in the night. This time it was to protect us from the latest deadly virus, the Backdoor Intruder.

Once again we dutifully worked through the update process with the standard issues regarding losing the internet for a while, and having the computer be convinced for several hours that we were a direct danger to its security and well being.

Contact your provider, it offered as a helpful solution. We have since learned that our provider had been sold to a conglomerate shell corporation based in Uruguay.

Eventually we were able to go back to eating our breakfast and staring at the monitors. There was no conversation of course, except for the infrequent announcements of various keenly important headlines.

"Looks like those politicians did it again," mused my wife. My reply was the standard, gracious, "Uh huh, what a bunch of idiots."

Boomer life was playing out just as we had expected.

Now that we had time to think about it, we also recently dumped our cable TV service in favor of hooking up a service called Roku, which apparently allows the streaming of various programming options through the TV via the internet, or possibly heaven.

We paid the new charges gladly because it was a slight net savings and it allowed us, on occasion, to avoid the pervasive barrage of insipid commercials experienced every four minutes on the live TV channels.

However, two weeks into the service, we realized that the new content contained an even larger barrage of insipid advertising breaks, in addition to the same batch of old ones.

Then there was the issue of our cell phones. After a noble round of due diligence we bought the Sing-Song brand, avoiding at all costs the notion that we might have finally allowed ourselves to be absorbed by the evil Apple empire.

The shouting matches and near divorce weren't really necessary, we finally decided.

When we turned on our new phones for the first time, the screens proudly told us to say hello to *your new life companion.*

Now wait just a darn minute! briefly coursed through my head about the tag line, as I began playing Angry Birds.

Naturally there was the GPS as well. Ah, the amusing stories we could tell about the time that Dorothy (we named it, of course) led us far astray, mispronounced a street name, or directed us up some populated stairway, and the time it faithfully guided us through a swamp.

Now we can't really go anywhere without it. In fact, yesterday I used it to find the garage.

There are dozens of other technological marvels throughout our home. A few nights ago I went downstairs in the middle of the night and noticed that every room in the house looked like the bridge of the Starship Enterprise, complete with a full array of blinking green and red LED lights.

You may have noticed a certain theme hinting at a slight discomfort with all the chip-driven tools that we have adopted into our daily lives. This, however, could not be further from the truth.

In fact, I recently fully embraced Sing-Song's marketing advice, and have named my new life companion Hermione. I haven't seen my wife in weeks.

Should we be concerned?

Maybe just a little?

My thought is that soon we will all be implanted with chips in our heads that will eliminate the need for learning the multiplication table and conjugating verbs. And it will select our breeding partners based on DNA testing tied to some kind of genetic hotness index.

The end state may be that, eventually we will all be just brains in jars as presented in most sci-fi movies. Maybe they can reuse some of the jars.

However, ever hopeful, there may still be a future for some of us if drastic actions are quickly taken:

Technology Reduction Ideas for Everyone

- Stop naming your appliances.

- Look up from your screen at least once a week. This will be difficult for many. Start with shorter periods of time for the first few months.

- You don't really need your GPS to find the bathroom. Just go.

- When you text while you are driving through an intersection, abbreviate.

- Only use lewd emoticons in every other sentence when contacting your pastor or probation officer.

- In the rare instance that your phone actually rings - run.

- Tablets make great coasters.

- Consider taking away your pet's laptop, or at least restricting the broadband gaming.

- At least once a week nod briefly to a family member. This of course includes your Sing-Song.

- And if all else fails, when tomorrow's new fatal technology virus hits - don't reboot.

In any case, don't worry about us. We finally solved our personal technology crisis. Living here on this uninhabited island in the middle of the Mississippi river hasn't really been all that bad.

We moved here after we accidentally clicked on an email advising us that we had were entitled to a huge inheritance from a distant family member in Nigeria. We probably should not have sent the $5000 administrative fee and provided all of our financial and personal information, including our belt sizes.

We lost the house, our bank account, our 401K, and all the rest of our personal possessions and assets. The brief jail time when we were arrested for supposedly buying two large yachts in Eastern Europe wasn't so bad.

In fact, life is better now than it has been for a very long time. We eat catfish and some kind of swamp weed every day. We wave at the tourist paddle wheelers as they go by, and have invented a full contact version of Go Fish.

And an unexpected side benefit is, now that our grown kids can't find us, we haven't been asked for money, babysitting favors, or bail bonds for weeks.

The batteries on our dog's tablet finally ran out and now Scooter plays with the family again.

In fact, you might say that finally we are no longer *technology's bitch.*

May you be so lucky.

Part 3

Boom Time

15

Travel

Best Places

The water rushed past the beleaguered rafting crew and howled in defiance as we hurtled through the narrow canyon. Our guide clung to the rear of the raft in a frantic attempt to keep the boat and the passengers upright, and between the rocks on either side. Huge waves pummeled the small craft as if they were determined to end us all.

Our helmets and goggles seemed barely enough protection and pinched like an army of evil insects as we gripped the rubber seats, and the spray pounded us relentlessly.

"Almost through," shouted the intrepid guide. "Hang on! No matter what!"

And then we were through. The water calmed. We reluctantly unclenched our hands from the sides of the raft, and smiled to each other, just glad to be alive.

"Well, that wasn't so bad, was it?" commented our leader. "Next time we'll actually put the raft in the river and try it for real."

It was the beginning of another great adventure.

Ask any Boomer and they will tell you that travel of some kind is on their bucket list. Rich or poor, healthy or not, most retirees long to see the world, or at least some small piece of it as part of their new work plan.

Some Boomers adopt the snowbird model, in which they live in a cooler climate in the summer and a warmer one in the winter. The concept makes perfect sense, as long as the relatives have no idea where to find you when you do it.

Other retirees buy a motor home or a trailer and make it their primary residence. There are some great clubs out there that add a much appreciated social aspect to this type of traveling. Consider having your next losing casino visit only a few steps from your living room. And you can always be first in line for those happy hour party wieners.

Also, we have heard that Wal-Mart actually lets you park your rusting motor home or trailer in their parking lot for as many days as it takes them to notice you and then kick you off their property. Sweet!

Here is some well researched input regarding the selection of great travel locations to see before you die.

The list may surprise you. Enjoy your visits!

Bucket List U.S. Travel Highlights

- **The Great Salt Lake** - Yes, it stinks in the summer, freezes over in the winter, only brine shrimp can live in it, and it has no water based activities of any type. It is really big and we have heard that you can float, usually without drowning, because of the toxic salt and silt concentration. Best enjoyed at thirty thousand feet.

- **Wall Drug, South Dakota** - Well, to be honest we've never really been there. However, they have put signs along the freeways all over America telling you how far it is to get there. Someone said there is even a sign in South Africa. It sounds great. Also, it appears that you can get some drugs there, maybe even marinara!

- **New Orleans, Louisiana** - Even after the hurricane several years ago, this great city is still a major attraction, particularly during Mardi Gras. We recently had a great time there watching the parades, during which mounds of garbage piled up on the sidewalks while flatbeds of drunken revelers with funny hats threw things into the crowds. The young women appeared to be catching all the beads for some reason. At one point I took a doubloon in the forehead, requiring several stitches. All part of the fun.

- **Denton, Texas** - At the local university, the sports team is named The Mean Green. Enough said.

- **Virginia City, Nevada** - Mark Twain went there once during a time in which some silver was mined, causing shootouts in the streets. All the residents eventually died, of course, and were buried in separate graveyards based on their race or if they were prostitutes. We took the tour.

- **Death Valley, California/Nevada** - Go in the summer to avoid the crowds.

- **Lookout Pass, Idaho** - This high mountain attraction, with its steep, narrow roadways and sheer drop-offs is best enjoyed in winter. Be sure to wave at the overturned trucks and motor homes. As a note, there is no cell phone reception there, so if you plummet over the edge, it may be a slight issue.

- **Buford, Wyoming** - Famous for being the smallest town in America. However, if you go there, it won't be the smallest anymore. We have heard that there is hot coffee sometimes.

- **The Everglades** - We loved picking up the poisonous snakes, lizards, and frogs. We bought a pair of water moccasins but they don't fit very well. And we even paid twenty five dollars to wrestle the alligators at the roadside attraction. I did get a small bite that took an arm. The manager said it sometimes happens, and gave me a coffee mug. Good times.

- **Washington D.C.** – Best travel site in America for attending endless comedy routines and side shows. Keep your wallet in an inside pocket.

A key to any travel experience is to always have a purpose or a goal tied to the places that you visit. Some Boomers make a list of interesting landmarks and sites within a city, usually based on the number of slot machines involved. Others want to enjoy the local sports or outdoor venues such as roller derby marathons or poodle races.

We are partial to maximizing our travel value in a city based on the brands of boxed wine and discounts received during happy hours as recommended on Yelp.

We have learned on our travels that, in the larger cities, some high end steakhouses and brothels offer a special menu in the early afternoon or late in the evening that dramatically discounts its regularly very expensive cuisine and adult beverages. Usually day old tacos are involved.

Once we ate twelve lobsters because they only cost two

bucks each. It only happened once though, because shortly after the incident our doctor told us we had achieved some kind of record regarding cholesterol.

He also mentioned that the shellfish may have been somewhat past their pull date due to the massive parasite infestations in both of us that also surpassed some prior medical achievement.

Then of course there was the tanker truck of merlot incident, but that is a story for another time. Good travels to you.

16

Travel

Getting There is Half the Fun

The big rig hurtled down the interstate in the fast lane. There was quite a bit of traffic at this time of the afternoon, and the destination city was still hundreds of miles away.

The driver was on a mission, it seemed. The fully loaded vehicle swayed and tilted in one direction and then the other as it plowed forward into the busy day ahead.

"Hey little buddy, got your ears on?" crackled the overhead speaker in the cab. "Just passed your spot and there's a bear at your back door." It was an important piece of news because there may have been just a bit of a speed issue as the rig tailgated some old guy going only five over the limit in the hammer lane.

"That's a 10-4 good neighbor." The vehicle slowed, efficiently moved over into the exit lane, and quickly left the freeway, leaving Smokey effectively trapped in traffic a few car lengths behind. "Think we'll head off and go through the woods."

The driver was getting tired in any case. He had been on the road for several hours and was beginning to feel the need to stop and rest for a while. He needed to pee.

The GPS noted that there was a diner a few miles up ahead. That would be a welcome sight.

As the vehicle neared its destination he blew a long blast

on the horn, just because he could. "Why travel if you can't have any fun!" he shouted to no one in particular as he pumped his fist in the air.

"What's that dear?" filtered in from the back of the aging Winnebago.

"Oh never mind," replied the gray haired Boomer to his sixty-something wife. "Have you seen the Tums?"

Their motor home, or road whale as many of their friends had lovingly dubbed it due to the large, poorly drawn picture of a whale painted on the side, slowed as it entered the diner's parking lot.

There was a huge sign on the front of the building that read *Eat Here - Get Gas*.

A hand drawn poster in the front window boasted Today's Special - Sushi! Featuring Rocky Mountain Oysters! He thought, *Yum*.

The intrepid travelers emerged from the rust involved Winnebago and hoisted the giant sun visor, with a graphic of sun glasses and a comical tongue printed on it, into place as they had done hundreds of times before.

"Let's eat," said his wife. "I have a craving for some blow fish. And oh look! The day old sushi is half price!"

Boomers have a unique perspective on traveling. The days of having children in tow or having to do some kind of business while on the road are long gone. It is a time in which there is, well, time to enjoy traveling.

This being said, there are many considerations still with which to contend. By this we mean you need a bunch of money to travel.

Even the most frugal Boomer needs to eat and sleep at some point. Often this includes finding lodgings for the night. In a perfect world it is best to find a place to sleep where your wallet is still somewhat intact the next morning, both in the cost of the lodgings and not having it stolen.

In this regard it is often best to avoid hotels or motels that include Bedbug or Hourly Rates in their signage.

Also rooms that rent for less than five dollars a week should be inspected before agreeing to stay.

Finally, be sure to pass up places with yellow police tape surrounding the courtyards and lobby. Also, if there are police cars, fire trucks, and more than one ambulance staged in the parking lot with lights flashing, move on.

Where to Stay

Handy Hotel Index

- Chain Hotel - Huge; expensive; impersonal; charges for parking and pillow mints; has an attached Hooters or Denny's; has a functional pool for the two weeks at the end of July.

- Independent Hotel - Moderately huge; less expensive than a chain hotel due to savings realized through spotty cleaning practices; no pool; has a Burger King down the block.

- Local Motel - Looks closed but isn't; paint probably looked okay when new before the big war; former pool is now an inadvertent reptile farm; usually has Bedbug or Hourly Rates in its name; next restaurant is one state over.

You're welcome! These helpful facts will assist you in planning your next stay at one of the major chains, or at that quaint roadside bed and breakfast. The key is to never look in, on, behind, or around any furniture or object in any of the rooms. And, just in case you get surprised, we've been told that bed bugs actually make great pets.

Sleep well.

Going Home

When traveling as a Boomer, one day you'll wake up and decide that you are tired of waffles poured out of a paper cup. You'll have forgotten the name of your hotel and the town in which it resides.

Most of the nearby bars with happy hours will have pictures of you on the wall announcing limits to your specific behavior involving the volume that you consume of the free appetizers and dollar beer. Some of the images of you will feature that red circle with a line through the middle.

Your travel mate will be down by the pool again, after having negotiated the appropriate compensation for the loss of the hotel's giant blow up gorilla that went missing during your last visit to the pool area.

Apparently those security video cams really do work.

It is also at this point that you will recall that you should have made arrangements before you left for someone to feed your former hamster and goldfish.

Consequently, later that day you decide to start the long trip home...

...via the route through the wine country, of course.

After all, it is only a detour of nine hundred miles.

17

Travel

About Wine

The treacherous mountain pass was one of the highest thoroughfares in the country. At well over eight thousand feet, with its twisting, winding turns and steep inclines, it was often referred to as The Deadman by the few travelers willing to attempt the transit. Although it was early fall, it was snowing. High snow banks still bordered the sides of the highway, having been created by the army of plows always at the ready in their often futile attempt to keep the area open to traffic. A thick layer of slick ice sparkled and taunted on the road surface. It was twenty degrees Fahrenheit, the high of the day.

The driver whistled and slapped his hands against the steering wheel to the far too loud country music song blaring on the radio. His huge tanker truck, completely loaded, was going a bit too fast for the conditions. At least that is what any normal person would have concluded. It was the last part of the run, and the highway tilted steeply downward toward the vast flat farmland far below. Road signs flashed and cautioned with their yellow and red warnings to all who dared the passage.

Stop! Go Back! Do Not Attempt! disappeared behind the tanker as it sped underneath the brightly lit overhead warning array.

Suddenly the driver stopped whistling and turned off the radio. Something was not right. He had just entered the steepest portion of the pass on the downhill side. He applied the brakes.

Nothing happened.

He pumped his feet against the brake pedal as it flopped uselessly on the floor of the cab. The truck was in fact now beginning to speed up.

The driver was frantic. What could he do? He vaguely remembered a runaway truck ramp somewhere on this stretch of road, but he could not recall where it might be. Then far ahead in the distance, a small flashing light on the side of the highway indicated...something. Yes, it was surely the ramp. The truck continued to increase in velocity as it careened around another set of sharp turns. Maybe he would survive, maybe not. It had been a good life in any case.

As the full tanker truck neared the ramp, the driver quickly looked at his watch. Wow! He was really late for his delivery. *Oh Crap!* he thought to himself as he prepared to plow into the steep sandy incline. He gripped the wheel tightly and...kept driving.

Not long after, his rig tilted on a turn and nearly tipped. He compensated, and the truck stabilized once more as the liquid in the tank sloshed and vibrated. Thankfully, his load this time was neither flammable nor caustic. The valley floor magically appeared through the windshield as he hurtled forward. The speed finally began to diminish as the highway flattened. He turned his radio back on and began to whistle once more. Damn the brakes. All he needed to do was put it into a lower gear. His delivery destination was just ahead.

As the driver backed the huge tanker against the loading dock and began to attach the hoses to transfer the cargo, the business owner appeared at the door. "It's about time John! Now just where the heck have you been with my load of Merlot?" Happy hour is almost over and we just ran out. I had to break into the good stuff to keep that unruly army of Boomers in the bar happy. Happy, get it?"

John finished unloading. His hands were still shaking from his recent ordeal. He had survived! He walked, gripping the handrail, to the entrance of the bar and headed inside. "Hi John!" shouted the large group lined up at the free wiener buffet. "What the heck took you so long? It's Boom Time!" Thankfully there were still fifteen minutes of happy hour left, and a few weenies.

The next day John got the brakes on his tanker repaired.

Wine Tasting Basics

All Boomers drink wine.

When Boomers come of age they are issued an official badge with a picture of a wine glass on it. It is expected to be worn at all times. Beer and hard liquor are also marginally acceptable, of course, but only when they cost less than a dollar a bottle or glass.

Now, we will admit that our definition of wine in this context may be somewhat skewed due to the fact that, in many cases involving our personal consumption, actual grapes were not part of the product's ingredient list nor preparation. However, we have read several glossy brochures on the subject, and even visited a winery once.

Let's walk through the basics:

Types of Wines

- Red
- Sort of red
- Pinkish
- White
- Sickly Sweet
- Unknown Blend (color varies)

Wine Taste Undertone Index

- Berry (black, straw, rasp, or Chuck)
- Unnatural (tobacco, leather, glue, brimstone)
- Gasoline/Lighter Fluid
- Other (licorice, anise, anise/licorice, beer)

Understanding Wine Labels

- Vintage: Year the grapes were picked, or Month in the price range Boomers can afford

- Award points: not applicable (see above)

- Marketing phrase about the vintner's flight from some oppressed land a few weeks ago

- Graph showing the dry/sweet balance, or for wines in the Boomer price range, a statement championing the fact that no one has died recently from drinking the particular product as far as they know

- Wine name: cleverly created by the winemaker after drinking heavily (ex. Marilyn Merlot)

Advanced Wine Skills

You are now well on your way to experiencing your first successful and emotionally gratifying wine tasting. There is even the possibility that you may remember a few of the details the next morning. Soon, you will be ready to progress to some more advanced wine tasting skills. For example:

- Telling the difference between wine and some other kinds of liquids

- Pronouncing Gewürztraminer (yes, that's how they spell it)

- Learning to impressively leave the "T" sound off of Merlot and Cabernet

- Performing the exotic art of swirling and spitting

- Implementing occasionally successful strategies for backing your car out on those long, one lane dirt roads encountered at all wineries, after another extended tasting

- Avoiding the use of a corkscrew on twist caps

Remember, the experts make the intricacies of wine attributes and tasting seem easy. But for now, if you can handle the basic skill of determining which end of the bottle to open, you are well on your way.

Consider the Boomer's wine slogan as words to live by:

After the first six glasses, there is no such thing as cheap wine.

18

Pets

Your First Ferret

The woods were dark and foreboding this late in the evening. We were miles from the car, and the thought of another Sloe Gin Fizz back at home in front of the fire was just a distant memory. There was a foot or more of snow on the ground.

Suddenly I saw the paw prints leading up to a dark cave above the tree line. "We got him now," I called out to my wife who was huddled against a rock outcropping overlooking the thousand foot drop.

Ever helpful, she mused, "I told you this would happen again. What part of close the gate is so challenging?"

Sure enough, Scamp was right there, deep in the back of the dark indentation on the steepest side of the cliff...and he wasn't alone.

Well, there were a few more steps involved in retrieving our pet full grown grizzly bear. Let it be said that we may have made a bit of an impulse move when we first brought him home from Pet Mart. He was just so cute.

Since then we have opted for smaller pets in general, except for that one anaconda related slip up, but that is another story.

We hadn't considered a ferret for a pet until we saw one frolicking on the shoulders of the lead pirate, pointing and waving at some perceived enemies, in the late night swashbuckler movie on television. The pirates won.

Early the next morning we were at the local pet store in an attempt to get a ferret for ourselves. When we arrived a clerk pointed to the back of the store next to the door into the loading area. There were two large cages currently inhabited by a few of the small critters. We considered getting a tame one from the first cage, but noted that they were a dollar more than the feral ones housed in a much smaller, more heavily wired enclosure behind some packing materials.

It was at this point that the store manager arrived at our side, out of breath. "They are on sale, you know." He said that today only, if you bought one of them you could get a second one for half price. We jumped at the chance and made the purchase. As we left the store the employees appeared unusually pleased with the sale for some reason. We could see them smiling, shaking hands, and pumping their fists in the air as we left the building.

Amusingly, on the way home, one of our new little weasel buddies escaped through the poorly secured door of its cardboard cage that had been included with the purchase. It climbed under the rear seat of our car and into the trunk. We must admit that the recapturing process was somewhat challenging, including more than a small amount of scratching, biting, and clawing. The ferret clawed a bit as well.

We named our new companions Frick and Frack. And although my first attempt at getting Frack to ride on my shoulders didn't go well, we remain hopeful.

Even better, since the mailman and meter reader incidents, we have yet to be served with restraining orders, lawsuits, or mailed death threats of any kind.

Yes, we have learned a few things about pet ownership, and thought it might be helpful to offer a few tips to those of you who have yet to pick up your first new Boomer style house buddy:

Selecting Your New Pet

- Poisonous reptiles make great starter pets, and they don't cost much. As a note, you may want to consider a cage or some kind of a pillow. Purina Lizard and Cobra Chow is recommended.

- Trolls don't make great pets because they are expensive to feed. Trust us, we know.

- Bunnies, chickens, mice, and hamsters are wonderful add on pets, particularly if you have opted for one of the options listed above. Buy several, but hesitate before naming them.

- Unicorns are fine but are very picky eaters, and our last one caused a fairy and elf infestation in our backyard that took weeks to clean up. Not recommended.

- For those of you living near water, whales make good pets, but sharks are much more fun, especially if you are near a swimming beach or wading pool.

- Some pets need to be kept mostly indoors. However, it is our understanding that kitty litter is far less expensive when purchased by the truckload.

- As previously noted, don't consider full grown grizzly bears unless you have a large back yard.

- Think tarantulas. Yes, they are marginally poisonous,

but we have been told that their teeth are far too small to get a good grip on you, unless they are trapped under your shirt or sweater. No problem.

- Golden geese make very good pets, but are often out of stock at the pet stores around the holidays.

Every Boomer needs a pet. Psychologists universally recommend them for enhancing personal health and family togetherness.

Most new pet owners agree that the fifty pounds of pet food that you must buy weekly is well worth the expense and back surgery. And many pets actually eat less after they are sixty years old or so, particularly if you have acquired a few auxiliary pets (see bunnies above).

Also, it is our position that vacations have always been overrated. Who needs them when you have a pet? If you really need to go to that casino or spa, you can easily find housing for your house buddy.

Pet hotels start at only two or three hundred dollars a night, plus the mandatory grooming, insurance, gourmet pet food, and yoga sessions. Hello Cancun!

The decision is an easy one, right? The next time you get that twinge of loneliness, driven by the fact that the kids moved out and you didn't leave them your forwarding address...think pet!

The mall beckons. Get something exotic. Get something big. Why wouldn't you?

Then again, as a last resort I suppose you could always get a dog.

19

Pets

About Dogs

The police car pulled into our driveway with its lights flashing. A stern faced officer emerged and headed toward our front door. Behind him, securely chained with a leash, tail wagging, was our two year old St. Bernard, Peanut. He was completely green, and was chewing vigorously on...something. "Woof," commented our faithful companion.

"We found him six miles away down by the dye factory," said the officer. "He was with a cute little poodle that ran off into the woods when we arrived. The guard dogs had him cornered and were about to have their way with him, we believe.

"We are not exactly sure how the green happened, but the plant manager said he will be talking with you shortly about his batch of premium custom ordered product being compromised by what he described as a significant drool incursion.

"And that thing he is chewing on appears to be the remains of the key to the city that the mayor was presenting to the ambassador from China at the park.

"A witness at the scene reported that, prior to the dye factory visit, your dog showed up at the town hall event.

"The ambassador, unfamiliar with our customs, apparently thought that playing fetch with your dog was part of the ceremonies.

"They say that the dignitary received some major licking abrasions, but will recover. The State Department will be calling you first thing in the morning."

As he climbed back into the car the officer then helpfully suggested, "And leave that gate open one more time pal, and you'll learn a new meaning for the word nightstick."

As we watched the tail lights fade in the distance Peanut looked up at me, dropped the chewed key, licked my now green hand, upgraded his tail wagging to furious, barked once loudly, and bolted through the still open gate and off again into the night.

People have pets, particularly dogs, for a variety of very good reasons. Pet lovers will tell you that the animals provide companionship for lonely Boomers, protect the property, and offer many other important values when they become a member of the family.

But, before you make a commitment to launch into full scale dog ownership, you may wish to consider a few interesting details involving your potential canine companion:

Your New Dog

- Dog size is important. Don't get a dog that you can step on, or one that can step on you.

- Don't pay any attention to the serving size noted on the bags of dog food. Research indicates that ALL dogs eat at least one hundred pounds of food per day, in addition to the pies, expensive cheeses, and prime cuts of meat stolen off the kitchen counter, and that your dog will subsequently poop, sometimes outside, twice that much.

- While shedding enough fur hourly to make a large sweater, your dog will bark relentlessly at cats, cars, rocks, and invisible aliens, even in their sleep.

- Burglars and home invaders are considered wonderful potential playmates by most dogs, while meter readers, mail carriers, and visitors from your church are on the bite first list.

- Dogs will eat anything, but prefer items that are priceless, poisonous, highly breakable, explosive, being placed on the Thanksgiving dinner table, or made from indigestible plastic.

- Your veterinarian expense will generally exceed your annual income (see above). Remember that your dog will only become sick in the middle of the night on Sundays, resulting in double extra overtime after hours vet costs for the pleasure of having the tennis ball removed - again.

- Heavy drooling is a requirement for all dogs. They are trained shortly after birth to achieve maximum volume and coverage.

- Dogs love to chew on the few items that they won't actually eat. Favorites include new furniture, car keys, designer dresses, your will, your paycheck, your Xbox, your cell phone, and you.

- You will regularly forget to close the gate. It is important to note that your dog has been spending every waking moment waiting for these glorious opportunities to escape their perceived imprisonment in your warm house and safely fenced yard. Just remember that your dog will always be able to run faster than you.

- As time permits, look up neutering in the dictionary.

- You can still consider a family vacation during your tenure as a dog owner. Pet hotels and boarders are readily available for only a few hundred dollars per night. Please note that during his visit your dog will have acquired a new, interesting, and complicated health issue each time, usually involving some kind of worm.

- Yes, all dogs are small and very cute when you first see them in the cardboard box in front of your local Wal-Mart. This is the time to remember that this particular dog will weigh a few hundred pounds when fully grown, only weeks after acquisition, and that your pet will become what the experts describe as a picky eater, being willing to starve to death if you don't provide that canned dog food with the gourmet chef in the big hat on the label.

- Although most dogs are reported to have a lifespan that is significantly less than yours, they will always live just long enough for you to be denied housing at your eventual nursing home.

There are many wonderful and fulfilling reasons to own a dog. We really do get that, and are completely in favor of the concept.

However, we highly recommend that it is finally time for your grown kids to be honored with the full time responsibility and ownership of the family dog. This way you can get the full tail wagging, licking, drooling, car key eating, and yard leaving experience any time you want. Then you can get back in your car, drive away, and go back home. You can even go on vacation if you get the urge.

If you don't have any grown children, maybe you should consider renting a dog for a couple of days a month from Hertz Rent-a-Drool.

Dogs can bring joy and companionship into every Boomer's life, if you understand and are willing to philosophically sign the long term contract.

If you do consider getting a dog, you may want to turn around in a circle three times before you decide.

20

Pets

About Cats

There's that human again, thought Supreme Goddess over all Things in the Universe. That was the name she had given herself, of course. The humans had originally named her Fluffy Boots, but that just seemed wrong to her.

At the moment she was hanging upside down near the top of the shredded remnants of the living room curtains. *I will say one thing,* she pondered, *they do have an excellent eye for quality fabric. This hand woven silk shreds beautifully, just like the last time.*

She presumably would have been inspired to pursue more personal comments about the current status of the previous draperies, but there was movement in the corner of the room. *MOUSE!*

The cat bounded off the curtains, tearing a long line of material off of the newly purchased sofa below. Then she scratched large grooves into the recently refurbished hardwood floor in the dining room, hell-bent on her important mission. *MOUSE!*

The presumed appetizer appeared to be attempting to find a way out of the corner of the laundry room behind the dryer. The human was frantically trying to follow the cat on her quest.

Needing some sustenance, the cat raced after the mouse. Earlier that day Supreme Goddess had rejected her morning meal again. After all, she had eaten filet mignon just the other day and was tired of it.

She reached the corner where the small gray critter was hiding and began ripping at the drywall. Nearby, a pair of designer jeans got in the way and she made quick work of them.

The meal then headed quickly for a small hole under the water heater. *Say goodbye buddy*, thought the cat, as she inadvertently raked the hot water hose and the thermostat from their sockets.

Seconds before the cat was prepared to pounce, the mouse looked up, and what may have been a smile flowed across its whiskered face. In a flash the mouse then expertly disappeared into the hole, just in time.

Crap, thought the cat, and she would have thought more if it weren't for the emerging fur ball that she hacked up. It was now covering the pair of satin high heels on the shoe rack.

It was precisely at this moment that Dufus, the family's pet schnauzer, spotted Supreme. He had just served himself an additional breakfast of coffee grounds and other unidentifiable morsels from the garbage can, and was concerned that the cat may have aspirations of sharing some of the remaining delicacies.

The expected chase ensued, lasting well over half an hour, and covered every square inch of the house and yard. Eventually the dog forgot the original reason for the chasing event, remembered that he had buried a bone somewhere at some time last year, and began digging for it in the kitchen.

The cat wandered slowly back toward her pillow-bed in

the master bedroom, stopping only briefly to poop in the recently cleaned hot tub. At the moment, the human seemed concerned. It was always hard to tell.

The newly damaged grandfather clock in the hallway chimed 8:00 AM.

Cats make wonderful pets, particularly for Boomers, or so we have been told by one of our friends who once knew someone who had one. We couldn't agree more.

The ancient Egyptians revered, and even worshipped them, believing they were reincarnated plumbers or insurance salesmen.

Archeologists have, in fact, excavated a large number of mummified cats entombed side-by-side with their human companions, presumably to comfort them in the afterlife. An alternate theory suggests that surviving family members simply used the opportunity to rectify a significant over population of the previous cat lover's feline menagerie.

In any case, the relationship between humans and cats has been around for a very long time.

Pets are an important part of life as a Boomer. After retirement, the social situations that were automatic while working begin to dissipate.

Having a furry buddy by your side can add years to your life, and can make life more interesting in general. Just be sure you take the time to pick the right buddy.

Things to Know About Cats

- They have the potential to be an excellent defense against rodents and other small household pests (armadillos, parakeets, spiders, relatives), if they could actually ever catch one.

- They provide much appreciated homes for fleas, ticks, and various worm species, which they are happy to share with your family.

- They purr. Scientists tell us that, although they cannot be completely sure, the purring was developed in prehistoric times to mean *you're next*.

- Cats will eat almost anything...that costs more than twenty dollars per small can. Most cats love Whole Foods brand Platinum Label Mouse Slaw with Gold Leaf Flakettes, except on Fridays.

- Kids love cats, until they try to touch or get near to one of them.

- Scientists have confirmed that more gets deposited in your cat's litter box than the cat originally ate. They are not sure why.

- Kittens are just the cutest thing ever, for about a week.

- Cat scratch fever is more than a song.

- Hissing, clawing, howling, and hackles mean love is in the air, or we should say the alley.

- You know your cat hates you, right?

Outside your local Wal-Mart is a basket full of multi-colored little cats (see kittens above). Your grandkids will have seen them on the way in, and you will have been subjected to a bizarre sales pitch (berated, pestered, threatened, coerced, and a few other choice interrogation tactics made popular by Genghis Khan) for the last half hour.

"No," you say.

"No! No! No! Never ever! Not ever! No cats! Not in my house! Not in my lifetime! Where is your mother?"

"But we promise to feed it when we visit, Grandpa! Please?"

"No cats! Ever!"

As you complete checking out with five hundred dollars of cat paraphernalia in your cart, and your new pet is already scratching the seat back fabric in your car, you wistfully wave to the grandkids driving away with their mother in the distance.

Now that your new houseguest has graciously allowed you to be its pet, there are a few more things you will need to know about it.

For example, all of the many days that your cat has suddenly and randomly disappeared are not happenstance. There are chapters around the country of a secret society known only to your cat that requires its attendance on a somewhat regular basis.

At these meetings they discuss the locally collected data on your personal habits, hygiene, intimate practices, friends, and other potentially destructive information for possible use at a later date. This evidence is stored in the off-the-grid Master Feline Incriminating Data Collection Archives headquartered in Arlington, Texas.

When your cat suddenly reappears shortly after you

were certain it was dead, presumably having been eaten by a coyote or a squirrel (who also have secret societies), you will surely observe a subtly enhanced swagger that lasts for several days.

We are certain that this directly relates to the rituals and practices that took place at the most recent event. However, we subsequently have been instructed by our attorneys that some interesting data has apparently been acquired from an unnamed source about the authors of this document, and to not discuss the details or *we'll be sorry*.

For those of you who have a cat as a pet and love it to death, please know that we are only joking about all of this, right? Cats make great companions for those of you who are willing to consider the occasional sideways glances from your across-the-room companion.

No wait, we really mean it. Cats make great pets. Please report to Fluffy Boots that we said this. This is very important.

21
Activities

Quilting

The radio host advised once more that it was minus ten and falling. The snow blew against the windows of our car at a fierce velocity as we angled down the steep mountain pass. It was hard to determine the depth of the blowing drifts on the road, but I had guessed a foot or more a few miles back. Still it came down with a vengeance.

Eventually, far in the distance lights appeared as a glow on the horizon. Every few miles we encountered a new barrage of flashing lights as rescue crews forlornly attempted to extract overturned tanker trucks and buses from ravines and rivers. And still we drove on with only seventy more miles to go.

Finally, as dusk was well in play, we ventured into the city and then into the parking lot of the mall. Some of the stores were already closing or had closed because of the extreme weather. But still our destination beckoned.

We bundled into our thick multi-layered clothing and navigated the icy concrete. I fell just twice, once into the open sewer in which water would have rushed if it had not been frozen long ago. No issue really. My injuries only included a severe sprain augmented by whiplash and a minor concussion. We trudged onward.

The fierce neon lights shined ahead. The automatic doors tried to open, and would have without the snow blockage. After some digging and prying we entered the store. "We'll be closing in six minutes," shouted the haggard looking clerk behind the fabric counter. We had arrived at The Quilt Store.

"I have a coupon," retorted my wife, as she raced to the back of aisle twenty nine.

Five and a half minutes later we were ready to pay. "That coupon expired yesterday," suggested the clerk.

Mall security was mostly helpful after they pulled my wife off of the store manager, and we were efficiently escorted to the waiting police car. Eventually we were released and carefully made our way back to our car, and then to the snow covered on-ramp in our necessary mission of somehow getting back home.

With the blizzard howling all around us, my wife protectively clutched the huge bag of fabric in her arms. She then defiantly and proudly proclaimed, "We got the coupon pricing! You're welcome."

My sling and crutches made it a bit challenging to drive, and we'd need to change the head bandages at the next rest area. It was midnight.

When we finally arrived home we needed to unwind a bit, and I was invited to watch another episode of The Antiques Road Show because they might be featuring a quilt of some kind. Some guy in an orange suit had just priced a damaged Cracker Jack toy at several thousand dollars.

Then they brought out a magnificent quilt that was over two hundred years old, pieced by pioneers who died in the act of making it, and hand stitched by the wife of a president. A different guy in a purple suit preached on for twenty minute about how this particular masterpiece was a treasure and part of our national heritage. He then proudly valued it at three hundred twenty dollars, but only if the current owner would spend a couple hundred more dollars fixing a small tear in the border. But I digress.

There still may be a few of you out there who haven't been introduced to the basics regarding the disciplines of quilting. For example, I recently learned that they don't use knitting needles. To assist your Boomer partner with their new crafting hobby, here are some helpful pointers:

Quilter Fun Facts

- Never attempt to query, look at, acknowledge, gesture, or make any sudden movements when your quilter is quilting. Ignore all comments about your family, personal attributes, or physical inadequacies. Only respond to direct threats or demands, and never make eye contact in any case.

- Fat quarters have nothing to do with weight or body size. They tell me that it's not personal. I learned this the hard way, I am afraid.

- Bobbins, Thimbles, Charm Packs, and Feed Dogs are more than just characters from Lord of the Rings.

- Quilters don't sleep, often for days. Something about one more block.

- A featherweight actually weighs quite a bit.

- There is something called a stash. It is different than the one you remember from the sixties that required a hookah pipe.

- When asked for your opinion...run.

- There is always one more trip to the local fabric store, and the store is always out of whatever is needed. Of course, the hundred mile store has plenty.

- There is evidence that all quilters secretly meet to discuss stitching patterns and world domination. No non-quilter attempting to learn more about this however, has lived to confirm it.

- There is batting, but no pitching or base running.

- Nothing in the house is safe from being quilted, or being connected in some way to the current mission. This includes the garage, attic, bathroom, and your dog.

During our last seemingly hourly visit to the local fabric store my wife immediately headed for the magazine aisle. For as far as the eye could see there were quilting magazines, each costing at least ten dollars. One cover helpfully suggested that you can solve that elusive gifting need with this hand-quilted full size Buick, with knitted V8 engine.

There was a whole shelf of magazines focused on Barn Quilts. *Wow! Imagine covering up a whole barn. Those things must be huge, and take a boatload of fabric,* I pondered. You would also need to be sure that the horses and cows get taken outside before installation.

Later that evening I detected my wife heading toward me with a huge collection of what appeared to be lumber under her arm and a big smile on her face. I tried to hide without success. She saw my feet sticking out from under the refrigerator. "It's called a quilting frame," she announced.

The construction plans were extensive and complex. However, some of the instructions were actually in what appeared to be some form of English.

After what seemed like several hundred dollars and almost as many parts, we were almost ready to begin construction. However, it appeared that one critical part was not to be found anywhere in town.

"I think I saw one of those when we were at the mall," she noted.

Before long we headed back onto the freeway. The temperature had fallen a bit to minus twenty, but the intensity of the snow storm had diminished somewhat. Of course, that may have just been wishful thinking.

We passed another row of flashing red lights hovering around an overturned Oscar Meyer Weiner Wagon. Sadly it appeared that one of the buns was damaged. We slowly edged around the scene, and anticipated that there would be more similar events along the way.

Finally, I could once again see faint lights flickering in the distance, as our journey continued into the dark night.

"Oh, and by the way," said my wife. "I have a coupon."

22

Activities

Deer Hunting (Inadvertent)

The trip down highway six toward Quincy was uneventful as usual. Dusk was approaching. We were halfway through the two hour transit to an actual city in which there was something called a mall. It had real escalators and a restaurant on the Mississippiissppi (check spelling) River with one of those famous Midwest all you can drink daily bar specials.

Suddenly there was movement on the road ahead. A deer bolted from the brush directly in front of our car. Other deer waited at the side to see if their buddy would make it across this time. The deer stopped and glared at us derisively, shaking and pawing the ground. I could tell by his or her expression that it wasn't the first time that this denizen of the woods had been in a similar situation. Then right on cue, the deer adopted the mandatory wide-eyed, official headlights posture and waited to meet its destiny.

Thankfully though, my uncontrolled and arbitrary veering and brake slamming maneuver worked perfectly, and tragedy was averted for us all. The bruising, whiplash, and abrasions we experienced would probably diminish in time, suggested my wife.

Looking back in the rear view mirror, I must admit it was the first time I had seen deer high-fiving each other on the shoulder of the road, but then we're not from around here.

When we returned home and shared the encounter with our friends, I expected several shocked affirmations and comforting retorts like "OMG! Are you guys okay?" or something similar, but they all just laughed and nodded knowingly to each other.

"Welcome to deer season," mused my former friend.

As it turns out deer season is apparently a very big deal in the Midwest. Every year thousands of Boomers, and some other people, descend on the area from all over the country with their favorite deer rifles, tanks, helicopters, and the occasional F-18 jet fighter, depending on the terrain, confidently expecting to bag their buck the first day.

At this special time, all Midwest towns proudly display huge bright signs announcing that hunters are indeed Welcome!

Banks sport electronic reader board signs touting things like Pump a Few Rounds of High Caliber Investments into our Vault. Jewelers offer Duck Dynasty engagement rings, and the local farm supply stores begin stocking pink (and blue, we're not sexist here) camouflage negligees and wedding dresses.

For those Boomers who are either new to the region or just passing through, here are a few tips and insights concerning this important time of year:

- Everyone must have a beard. This includes women and children.

- All footwear must include mud. Those needing starter mud can purchase a supply at Wal-Mart.

- Yes, camouflage is required at all times. This

includes your car and pets.

- It is understood that no one ever actually bags a deer. Artificial deer legs are available to have sticking up in the hunter's pickup bed while returning to town, to create the appearance of success. Antlers are available as well, but carry an upcharge.

- The one exception for failing to get a deer is through hitting one with your car on the way home from your hunting trip. If this occurs, shoot it postmortem and make up a great story about how it took hours of tracking, shooting from five hundred yards against the wind, etc.

- All pickup trucks must be at least twenty years old and formerly painted red. Heavy rust is also required for the fenders. Once again, rust can be purchased if needed.

- Embellishing the reasons for your lack of hunting success is essential. Prepare in advance several variations of your story about how the seven point buck was in your sights, but a rare bald eagle distracted you, and then the snake...and so forth.

- Shooting anything that vaguely resembles a deer is acceptable and even encouraged. Taking out the occasional tractor or Buick is just good practice.

- Drinking Budweiser is a must before, during, and after your hunting trip. It is even better if you can get the deer to drink one as well.

- Be sure to hunt only in areas that have chosen not to post No Hunting signs. For example, it is fine to hunt in the Burger King parking lot.

These are the basics that you will need to prepare for your next hunting trip. The key is to look like a hunter. Remember that designer camouflage is always available at bagmeabigone.com.

If by unexpected circumstance you actually happen to bag a deer, it is good to know that if you do the math, it will work out to no more than $89.00 per pound of usable venison when all is said and done...

...and if it weren't for the fact that the meat will have spoiled by the time you get it to the locker, it would certainly have been a great investment, and delicious as well.

We wish you success on your next deer hunting trip to the Midwest. Of course we won't be able to see you because of the camouflage, but we will see your truck sporting the legs sticking up out of the bed, or possibly the antlers.

Good hunting!

23

Activities

A Guide to Lawn Care

Long Ago

The ground shook. It wasn't just one of those pedestrian upheavals that take place during an earthquake registering 7.0 or 8.0 on the Richter scale. It really shook.

Unsecured objects near the event bounced high into the air, littering the ground with debris for miles in all directions. Villagers fell to the earth, curled up in little balls like tumbleweeds, and patiently waited. The shaking continued.

The huge beast that had caused the incident looked content. It spanned almost one hundred thirty feet from its nose to the tip of its tail. Its head was relatively small compared to the rest of the body, but the belly was huge. Beady little eyes scanned the lush grasslands which seemed to go on endlessly. The creature's mouth, which took up most of its head, appeared to turn up at the corners in a faint smile. It engulfed massive quantities of grass, along with collateral vegetation, boulders, and occasionally, distracted onlookers, in each bite.

It lumbered forward with purpose, as always, but at the moment appeared to have drifted off course a bit. Unfortunately, it was now walking with deliberation toward the village itself, and in fact, directly toward the opulently thatched hut of the chief.

A small figure could be seen walking by the side of the brontosaurus. He held a large whip in one hand and was furiously swinging it at one of the dinosaur's legs. However, it was clearly having no effect.

The ground shook once again. The village was now much closer than it had been a short time ago. The creature looked up for the first time. The thatched hut roofs beckoned. They looked delicious. The people who lived in the village also looked up and noticed the unusual activity. This wasn't supposed to happen.

In a final frantic attempt to stop the forward progress, the herder threw himself in front of the beast. He had worked with Bessie for years now and had what he believed was a great relationship. In short, he and Bessie understood each of their roles. Surely she would stop. There was a moderately loud crunch as the forward progress continued, and the herder disappeared beneath the swaying belly. The village chief surveyed the situation with increased concern.

Fortunately, with the loss of the herder, the great beast finally stopped and appeared perplexed. Clearly the situation was unstable at this point. Direct and swift action was definitely needed, the chief decided. It had been a while, but it was time to talk to Grunt.

Shortly thereafter, Grunt could be seen quickly approaching the outskirts of the village, leading a huge, toothy monster with tiny arms (the dinosaur's, not Grunts, although Grunt's arms weren't that big either). The T-Rex, whom everyone knew as Big Willy, roared. The ground shook even more than it had with the other beast, and just before the lumbering brontosaurus began to munch on its first thatched roof, it stopped again and looked up. *What the heck is that? Wow! Those arms are really tiny.*

The epic battle that subsequently ensued was recorded in tribal lore for generations. In the end, Bessie lost the fight, and the T-Rex also expired a couple of days later. As it turned out, in a serious tactical error the carnivore was badly out of position when delivering the fatal bite, and the brontosaurus landed right on top of it as it died and...well, you know. Grunt was also tragically lost during the melee, suffering a heart attack while trying to pull Big Willy out from under the other monster.

The village chief was relieved, but saddened. The herder, Bessie, Big Willy, and Grunt had been part of the village culture for a long time. The T-Rex, whose usual job was protecting the local population against attacks by other villages, was easily replaced, of course. There were lots of them in the canyon, and they were ironically simple to catch due to their tiny arms.

On the other hand, brontosaurs were rare, finicky, difficult to train, and - let's just go ahead and say it - not too bright. In this regard, the monumental problem and most disturbing issue triggered by this unfortunate event, was...

...what were they supposed to do now to get the village lawn mowed?

The luxurious expanse of meticulously maintained grassland surrounded the village for miles in every direction, and it was already looking shaggy. The unstomped, uneaten weeds had begun growing rapidly.

The chief morosely began the long walk into the canyon to find another bront. He was reluctantly joined by the pointy-spear-induced future herder and head landscape manager, whose nickname coincidentally was Little Willy. The large, red stained, and dinosaur littered grass area where the unfortunate incident occurred faded in the distance.

On the plus side, however, the village ate well for weeks.

Present Day

Your Lawn is Growing Right Now

Mowing the lawn is a critical part of becoming a Boomer. Sure, you mowed the lawn your whole life, but this is different. It is a rite of passage of sorts for the newly retired.

Finally, you have the time to think about mowing rather than just getting it over with every week. The process can now be moved from the *necessary but annoying* task list directly onto the *let's go mow the lawn again right now, it's only snowing a little* agenda.

There are many levels of mowing styles and options, of course. Consider for the moment the ultimate approach:

The 9000

The noise of the manufacturing equipment was nearly deafening. "Get those forklifts over to the blade fitting area pronto!" shouted the foreman, his hard hat tilted a bit too far back for real safety.

"The new shipment of military grade steel plating is here sir," said one of the loading dock leads.

"Thanks Jimmy. We'll deal with it as soon as the mucky-mucks finish their tour," responded the chief.

The work area was impressive and huge. Looking east you could almost see the far wall, with row after row of manufacturing equipment in between.

To the West was the massive storage facility which, some had claimed, housed every known part and service capability for this type of manufacturing.

However, at the moment all that the staff was thinking about was the fact that The Boss had just walked into the lobby of the sales pavilion.

The team of visitors had arrived, after landing in the corporate jet, in three of those golf cart type vehicles that you always see in James Bond movies.

"Over here is the secondary replacement parts section," said the glowing team leader. "We look forward to introducing you to The Unit," he proudly offered.

"Welcome aboard sir," said the foreman. "The prototype is ready for the demonstration that you requested, sir."

"Fine, that's just fine, Jacobs. Let's get on with it, shall we?" The now large group of hard-hatted managers headed purposely toward the testing arena located almost half an interior mile away.

"Well, here we are, sir," said the foreman. "Binkers, ARE YOU READY?" he shouted.

"WE'RE ALL SET BACK HERE," Binkers shouted back.

"God speed," was heard filtering in from the back of the crowd.

There was a huge lighted stage at the far end of the arena. Flashing strobes and an impressive pre-programmed set of colored lights began swirling to the rhythm of *Born to be Wild*, which had begun playing loudly in the background. The lights finally focused in on a covered platform in the center of the stage.

Suddenly the music and lights stopped, and the cover began to lift.

"Ladies and gentleman," intoned a deep, disembodied voice off stage. "Introducing to the world for the first time. They said it couldn't be done. Many laughed, and yet we persisted. Finally today we have made it happen for you! Please join me today in welcoming the Lawnmotivator 9000. One thousand inches of Harrier jet powered mowing magnificence!"

We are the Champions blared over the loudspeakers. The cover continued to lift slowly. The dozens of coats of gleaming paint flashed and sparkled. Everyone held their hands to their ears as the engines roared to life.

The crowd cheered wildly. The uninvited John Deere representatives who had been lurking in the back of the massive arena headed dejectedly for their car, shaking their heads in dismay.

A few months later, at a retail lawn and garden store thousands of miles from the factory, a proud, soon to be mow-master Boomer watched as they loaded his shiny new 9000 onto the waiting forty foot flat bed trailer.

"Grandpa," queried his young granddaughter, who was trying stay out of the way of the flurry of workers shouting important loading instructions, "Why do you need such a big lawn mower when you live in a condo?"

"It's all right there in the Boomer's Guide to Life Manual," he responded. "Someday you'll understand."

Your Mowing Profile

What kind of mower are you?

- **You Name your Lawn Mower Weedwrath** - You mow the lawn twice a week, every month of the year. Last December you got lost for three days in the backyard, but were eventually rescued. They have your picture up at the fire station next to several other pictures of cats as rescue of the month. Today is Weedwrath's birthday and you are on your way to buy that special weed-n-feed he asked for.

- **Farm it out** - You pay the kid next door five bucks to mow your thirty acre lawn, and then complain about the poor trimming job down by the largest of the three rock filled canyons.

- **The Joneses** - You won last year's cul-de-sac lawn competition going away, when you mowed an exact replica of the Mona Lisa into the front yard, reproducing the smile and the hidden satanic messages perfectly.

- **Master of The Plan** - Should I mow in concentric circles like that sheep in the kid's story, or diagonally like they do in professional baseball, maybe a checkerboard? Now if I could just get the lawn mower to start.

- **Fertilizer** - You waited a bit too long after fertilizing and haven't been able to mow since last April. You bought the really good stuff. Your lawn has grown several feet tall since then. Last week one of your grandkids disappeared in the foliage. You are still hopeful that he will someday be found.

- **Goats** - You buy some, then some more. The cul-de-sac committee files a formal complaint with PETA. You are arrested and eventually sentenced to prison after your goats accidently eat your next door neighbor's new Mercedes.

- **Hire a Pro** - You get several bids and hire the lowest bidder for only two hundred dollars per week to mow your yard. The workers arrive in several brand new Ford F-150's. They mow over your above ground swimming pool, prize winning roses, and one of your garden gnomes. As they drive away you notice that they have apparently forgotten to actually mow the yard. Elapsed time - five minutes. Later that week you receive a bill for two thousand dollars to cover lawn mower depreciation.

- **For profit** - You turn your yard into a putt-putt golf course complete with mermaids, windmills, and creepy clown holes. You go viral on YouTube when the clown topples during a windstorm and traps one of your customer's dachshunds for several hours, the dog ultimately being rescued when found inside the huge red nose. You earn millions and retire to Greenland, where they don't even have a word for lawn in their language.

- **Make it Stop** - Geez, I'm retired. No more lawns, weeds, dog poops, rocks through windows, unplanned bare patches, gas trimmer injuries, minced frogs, or near death experiences via mowing during lightning storms. Condo me!

Here in the Midwest most towns have a robust lawn mowing culture and economy. The small city in which we live, for example, has several lawn maintenance laws on the books.

Last year one of our neighbors went on vacation and their lawn grew past the eight inch maximum. When they returned, the lawn had been mowed and someone else was living in their house. Their appeal to the city council failed, and they were assigned eight weeks of poison oak removal near the land fill. The last we heard, they left during the night and moved to somewhere in Northern Canada.

Personally, we have had a few minor lawn code violations as well, the worst one being incremental toadstool proliferation. Consequently, we do admit that we have also thought about our residency options.

Today a book arrived in the mail that my wife apparently ordered. *Better than Greenland!* it read on the cover. *Start your New Life at the South Pole: No Bears! No Lawns! No Problems!*

Let the packing begin.

24

Activities

Everything but the Squeal

The row of street lights had just come on for the evening, and they sparkled through the mist as we walked toward the casual restaurant that bordered the parking lot of an aging gas station and strip mall.

We waved to the guy wearing a sandwich board with advertising for the gas station, as he danced on the curb across the street. He waved his arms wildly in frantic circles as he spun around and around, with his sign declaring "WE HAVE GAS!"

We walked on. The sound of conversation, clinking glassware, and the occasional shouts and laughter intensified as we neared our destination.

We entered the restaurant that was as familiar to us as an old shoe. The host led us to our usual seats in the bar. "There you go kids," she intoned. "Good luck."

Our server eventually approached.

"So, what's the special tonight Bethany?" I queried.

"It's a liver and onion omelet with a calamari glaze, whatever that is," she responded. "And you can get an option of frog legs on the side for an extra two dollars."

"Sounds delicious," we nodded. "Let's have that, except hold the liver, calamari, and frog legs. Hold the onions. Add a cheese burger and fries to the eggs, except we don't want any cheese, and no eggs."

"So the usual then," she responded, and walked away with purpose toward the kitchen.

We sat back in the darkened room full of Boomers who, like us, had clearly given up cooking any type of food at home, except for occasionally opening a bag of pork rinds.

The local news was on the television behind the bar with the sound turned off. We weren't sure what they were saying, but they looked pretty mad about something.

Country rock seeped into the room in the background. It was too early to use the juke box to buy long sets of heavy metal.

Our happy hour wine arrived shortly thereafter. They had just opened a new box! It was a good day to be alive.

In retirement it is important to maintain good nutrition. Even if you go out to eat twelve or more times a week, like we do, you can still select menu items that may be considered healthy in some cultures.

For example, chicken strips would have only a few hundred fat calories per strip if you were to order them without the chicken or breading. And salads are proven nutritional winners when you just get the lettuce.

In this regard we have prepared a few hints and tips for your next trip out to dinner:

- Salad bars are nothing like the kind of bar with which you are familiar. Salad involves things like kale and kelp.

- Try the pan-fried trollops.

- Use caution when ordering the daily special. Frugal chefs often use food items that didn't sell the previous day or week, and sometimes they add in fillers like shreds of something marginally meat-related, egg shells, or coffee grounds. They will disguise the contents by calling the dish Hunter's Mix or What Not or Skillet Surprise.

- Don't order anything with tentacles.

- Avoid dishes with names that include quinoa, gluten, or fiber. No one really knows what these things are.

- If you get excited by the phrase All You Can Eat, we're sorry.

- If you live in a state that allows All You Can Drink specials as well, we also feel like we should be sorry... but...

- Becoming a restaurant regular has nothing to do with your bathroom habits. However, if you order the special, all bets are off (see above).

- No matter how long the happy hour is at your particular restaurant, you will have always just missed it by five minutes.

- The early bird special rarely has anything to do with birds, but we have learned that it often has a lot to do with tentacles.

About the Menu

Restaurants spend a great deal of expense and effort in the preparation of their menus, focused on the food offerings and the way each dish is presented.

An example might be the latest trend toward including dishes comprised of unusual animals or parts of animals such as guinea pigs and bone marrow.

This has been made popular, of course, by the television reality shows where the host prides himself in eating something completely unrecognizable as a food, except for the fact that it is covered with blood. The native offering it up is always pointing towards his mouth and grinning.

The star of the show pops bits from the proffered carcass into his mouth, tentatively chews, and nods knowingly, as the villagers high-five each other and exchange money with the winners of the bet.

In fact, we feel worse for the producers and camera crews of these programs, who have to finish the mess to the last bite. After all, they wouldn't want to be disrespectful to the tribe once the host has taken his one bite.

It is our understanding that a few of these faithful, behind the scenes personnel are still alive, mostly living in protected homes and shelters.

Then there is the environmental component of the discussion. America is famous, of course, for wasting more food than it eats while people a mile away from the eaters starve to death. But that's a story for another day.

The rest of the world doesn't act this way, and food is

never wasted. Ask anyone, anywhere except here, and they will tell you that they eat everything but the squeal...and we applaud this.

However, that doesn't mean that the things that they won't use in hot dogs need to show up on your dinner menu described as a new taste sensation.

More about Menus

- Surf and Turf used to mean steak and premium seafood such as lobster. Now you must read the fine print to see if the description includes a sea cucumber on a bed of dirt (gourmet dirt, of course).

- Remember that soft shell crab is on the menu only because the chef couldn't figure out how to remove the shell. Also, it is certain that the kitchen staff enjoys watching you pretend that your labored crunching is natural and expected for this dish.

- Then there is the example of tiny food. This aberration certainly started as a joke in the big city markets, where media-made-famous chefs championed the idea that twenty one-bite dishes in a meal were worth the four hundred dollars that they charged. Amazingly (but nothing surprises us anymore) the customers loved it. If you see any reference on a menu to *tasting* or *molecular* - run.

- Speaking of molecular, you can now buy dishes in restaurants that literally smoke, fume, explode, or melt on your plate. Many of these are fashioned to look like eyeballs or other things found in nature, usually under rocks, to add to the experience. We now understand that one New York restaurant is actually serving rocks. But don't try to get in. There is a year-long waiting list.

- Be wary of some of the sauce and condiment descriptions on the menu. If the dish suggests that it includes an exotic blend of natural ingredients, or that it was locally grown, be aware that the basement of the restaurant has plenty of exotic and local things growing in it even as we speak.

- Tapas means "unsuitable for pets" in Spanish.

- Never order sushi at a gas station or McDonald's.

- Tasteless, inedible, or generally failed menu items that still have an ingredient inventory in the restaurant's freezer are often served in other configurations as *organic*.

- Small Plates is just another name for Tapas (see above).

- You've heard the joke, of course, about which part of the chicken is the tender, right? Sadly we must inform you that there are a few people in the kitchen of the restaurant that you are in right now who actually know the answer to this question.

- Remember that there is a guy sipping a tequila sunrise on a beach near his condo in Tahiti because he came up with the name Prairie Oysters.

In the Out to Pasture world, restaurants and bars are the Boomer's new best friend. All of your previous friends from your days of raising kids and working are dead now, or living in Las Vegas (same thing).

So, the next best option at your stage in life is to adopt a series of local watering holes, and attempt to make some new friends.

This, unfortunately, is not as easy as it sounds. There are usually a few other Boomers in the places you have chosen to frequent, but they often can't remember who they are, let alone who you are. And the conversations usually contain the words bladder or cramp.

You may attempt to engage with some of the other patrons in the bar who are younger, including your server.

It always starts out fine.

"Hello there Heather (she has a nametag). We'll have the prairie oyster appetizer, with extra prairie, please."

"Hello back at you," she responds. "Do you want the cheese sauce with your oysters?"

"You bet. And what do you suppose those things that are always floating in it are called?"

"Oh, those things aren't actually supposed to be in there, they tell me. Don't worry about it. They're dead."

"Are you a student at the college?" we mused.

"Uh huh," she said, making a note on the order to hold the floating things.

"What are you majoring in?" we asked carefully.

"I'm in my fifth year, majoring in communications, law enforcement, and public health, with a minor in animal husbandry," she responded.

"Wow, that's impressive. What are you going to do with that when you get out, except be a prison disc jockey working out of its farm hospital?" we joked.

"Yes, that's it exactly. I am interning already upstate," she said, walking away to put in our order.

The conversation ended at that point without any progress in regards to starting a new social relationship.

Another Boomer couple sitting next to us had heard most of our interchange. They looked over and smiled. "Having some cramping," commented the older gentleman." We offered them a bite of our oysters.

Heather was gone the next week, like most of the others. Last we heard, she had been promoted to on-air talent somewhere in New York, and now has her own talk show titled Beat it with a Stick. It is going into syndication.

The experts tell us that socialization is critical to a healthy, happy retirement. So, get out there and socialize. Order something new, from someone new, from somewhere new. Who cares if you'll need to get shots. Do it now.

The good news is that most restaurant food won't actually kill you, at least not right away.

25

Activities

A Shop on a Different Corner

The sound was deafening as the huge object hovered near our front porch. The Boomers in the neighborhood had quickly mobilized as a militia group to counter the certain invasion, presumably by Canada, and the women and children were lined up behind their hastily constructed bunkers. The men hid in guerilla combat mode behind the dumpsters. Glocks and AK47s bristled along the barbed wire that they had placed around the rose bushes. F22's and other jets screamed low over the horizon, afterburners engaged. The end was clearly near.

I had tried to tell my wife that this was not the best way to order delivery for a full sized cement mixer, but she wouldn't listen.

We had serendipitously noticed, while searching on the net for drain cleaner at three AM, that the C3750 Super Mix Blaster was on a Lightning Deal at Amazon.

"OMG! Look at that price," shouted my wife.

"But do we really need another cement mixer?" I countered. Then I saw the price.

"Wow, and they are including a reinforced digester and rubberizing at no extra cost." The order was placed with only minutes to spare.

In our haste we had apparently pushed the automated

delivery button, described as a great new shipping option, with no freight upcharge.

Be the first on your block..., the advertising on the ordering page persisted.

Well, now we knew exactly what the process entailed.

"Get down, get down," our next door neighbor yelled. "It's coming in for another pass. Fire weapons at will." The blasts were unbelievably loud as all rounds were discharged.

The delivery drone didn't even seem to notice. And moments later it settled on our front lawn, crushing a decorative pear tree and an unfortunate poodle.

Several large clanking sounds and the release of hydraulic fluids ensued, followed by a huge thud. Our mixer had been delivered.

The drone headed off towards the sunset with its next delivery. I could see a full sized Buick SUV dangling below the deck of the vehicle.

Somebody's getting a nice birthday gift, I pondered as the drone disappeared in the distance.

Slowly, the neighborhood returned to normal. Weapons were stowed and children began swinging from the remaining swing sets (the ones not blown over by the turbulence).

"That worked out pretty well," commented my wife. "And that two day drone delivery thing is great. Let's go take another look at today's deals. I think I saw big discount on refurbished jet engines."

We headed back inside.

When we were young shopping was easy. You'd grow, hunt, or build something, walk a few miles with some shiny rocks or clam shells, and trade for something that someone else grew, built, or hunted.

Later there were the local grocery, hardware, and department stores. There was the Sears Catalog.

And here we are today, in a shopping world sporting an endless array of things that can be had at a moment's notice, to satisfy even the most bizarre and arcane of our culture's invented wants and needs.

In this regard we offer these few hints and suggestions to maximize your shopping experience in the new century:

- Never buy frozen foods or party ice on the internet. The price points are usually not competitive.

- Do buy dentures or dental crowns online. We have found some exceptional offers and a wide variety of colors from which to choose.

- Remember, selfies are now a real thing. Buy them by the gross for best value.

- Never again waste resources on physical birthday or holiday cards. The net offers an unbelievable array of virtual singing, off-color, tasteless, and offensive options for this important purpose. We particularly like the Make a Sailor Blush series.

- Take extra time when selecting a tank or submarine. Pricing varies widely, and last year's models usually work just fine. Don't forget to factor in the freight cost, particularly when ordering from Moldova.

- Buying live animals from Amazon can be a bit tricky. We always go to the endangered species page first. Be sure to consider whales, or something from the poisonous reptile selection. These often make the best pets.

- Purchasing wine online has become very popular. Cheaperbythetankerload.com is now our favorite resource. We can't begin to tell you about the great deals we have gotten on less than pristine labeled truckloads of various types of tasty selections in red, white, and uncertain.

- Consider a fully stocked aquarium.

- Be sure to sign up for the Kindle digital book service. This way you can have a library of books that you will never read in a much smaller storage area. Your old paper books can be burned. We hear that they make great kindling, particularly the ones that don't have pictures.

- Locally, you can and should frequent the Big Box Stores. They have everything that you might ever need, including car insurance. Be sure to brush up on your math regarding measurements including drum, kilo, barrel, and pallet to better understand the minimum quantities that you will need to buy (even the insurance).

Everything that you have known about shopping has changed. In this new paradigm you can now move to a remote village on the tip of the Kamchatka Peninsula and still get deliveries in two days of anything that you can possibly dream up to purchase.

In addition, there is now a little person living inside your cell phone - just say, "Hello Satan." This disembodied voice will actually tell you what you need to buy, as recommended by a stable of D-list celebrities.

Finally, only about fifty percent of what you order will arrive broken, be the wrong item in some significant way, or will never arrive at all, for which you will be blamed. These are pretty good odds compared to the old days when you had to break most of the items yourself.

Yes, it is a wonderful world for Boomers to still be hanging around in, isn't it?

26

Activities

Understanding Professional Football

The crowd roared as first striker Quetzalcoatl bounced the heavy rubber ball off the wall and into his opponent's midsection. The ball then careened into the ring at the end of the stone court. It was the winning point of the game and he slapped hands with his teammates as the losing players were led off the field and up to the loser's consequence platform. The losing team did not look happy.

Somewhat later Soccer (yes, the Europeans cleverly called it football - but we don't care) became the standard for many years.

The game was similar to the Aztec game played centuries earlier, but players in the new sport used their feet and heads instead of their hips to move the ball around.

And apparently, human sacrifice was reluctantly abandoned over time, by most soccer teams anyway. The fans, however, continue the practice in many venues even today.

None of this matters of course, because after its invention no one ever actually watched a soccer game again, except as punishment for murder or swearing.

History tells us that, as the now wildly popular game of football subsequently evolved, the ball was initially intended to be round like its soccer ball predecessor. But there weren't that many ball makers in the new world who could actually make a product that remotely resembled that configuration.

There is documentation that, in a fit of despair, and with a quickly growing inventory of poorly constructed balls, one of the ball manufacturers drew up some rule changes for the new game on a cocktail napkin at the local pub.

The changes described requiring a hideously misshapen oblong ball, made from the hide of an unfortunate pig and sewn together with left over shoe strings, that was to be used in the game.

At first the sport was called Bad Bouncing on Purpose Ball, but after they sobered up, the inventors quickly saw the value of finding a different name that would help sell more beer.

Apparently the names Handball, Squash, and Illegal-Block-in-the-Back were already taken, so they quickly decided to call it football, ignoring the fact that this name was also taken and that feet would rarely be used at all in their newly invented game.

In the early days of football it was easy for the fans to be involved. You'd cheer for your local team The Anteaters at the stadium or landfill, maybe even wearing your replica black and yellow striped jersey that you bought from the Sears catalog for a dollar. Then you would mourn your team's inevitable loss by getting unbelievably drunk.

Then television was invented.

Today, Boomer's have plenty of time to watch and enjoy football, America's favorite sport (no, it is not baseball - deal with it).

However, with a rule book that has evolved over generations, this complex game that is still played with an oblong spheroid is not easy to understand anymore.

But thankfully for Boomers everywhere, we're here to help navigate the finer points of this great sport:

Picking and Watching Your Team

Thanks to satellite and cable television you aren't stuck rooting for your hometown team anymore. All you need to do is pay several hundred dollars a month to watch, from your sofa, your favorite millionaire celebrity wide receivers strut onto the field and drop easy catches.

The key to selecting your favorite team is simply based on the four Q's:

- The Quarterback

- Player Nicknames and Arrest Records

- Cheerleader Outfits

- Beer

In any case, your football watching money will be well spent as you watch your favorite team The Giant Squids, based in Kansas, lose again 3-76.

Commercials

There are those who joke that football broadcasts are now nothing more than an endless series of commercials, briefly and reluctantly interrupted by the game. Nothing could be further from the truth, my friend.

Yes, it is true that games scheduled to begin at one o'clock actually start at two o'clock due to the pre-game sponsored warm-up content. And that during the actual game *we'll be right back* breaks are launched after every play, at twice the volume used in calling the game.

But these interruptions are clearly useful and necessary in your game watching experience. And don't forget, one minute of those interruptions involves someone trying to sing the National Anthem.

Consider, for example, that the endless interruptions make it easy for you to get snacks, cook a turkey, have a wedding, or write a book between plays.

The fact that the three hour halftime show is now all commercials also facilitates your ability to build a new addition to your house or adopt a child during the break.

Note that all commercial breaks now exclusively involve drinking a particular brand of light beer (apparently resulting in dates with supermodels for the lucky drinker), male impotence, and previews of upcoming commercials.

Then there is the advertising scrolling at all times across the top, bottom, and sides of your screen. These solicitations tie the viewer's attractiveness to the opposite sex with the purchase of Official NFL Branded Products, such as hand guns and toaster waffles.

Of course, every sentence uttered by the announcers during the game will have an embedded sponsor reference as in the example, "Today's game ball is brought to you by Barely Bacon, Official Reconstituted Pork Rind of the NFL."

The Players

Football players have now been grouped into categories for easy reference. There are quarterbacks, players with dreadlocks, and players without dreadlocks. Some of these players play defense. This should help you as you are analyzing the plays on the field.

The Plays

There are four basic types of plays in football; short missed passes, really long missed passes, quarterback sneaks, and plays where one of the players tries unsuccessfully to run with the ball.

Strutting and taunting are also now required on every play, including those in which the player involved has made a huge mistake, turned the ball over, or injured one of his own teammates.

Sometimes there is touchdown, but the ball doesn't actually have to touch anything.

The End Zone Dance

When a touchdown actually occurs, the successful ball carrier is required to wildly gyrate, twerk, break dance, or careen across the end zone making obscene gestures.

Some players end up in the stands where inappropriate touching is expected and embraced.

Players found inadequate in performing any of these critical tasks are often penalized five yards on the upcoming kick-off, and given stern looks and demeaning eye rolls by the officials.

The Officials

This one is easy. Referees are charged with making a holding call on every play. They are also required to call pass interference when there is none, and to not call it when there is.

Occasionally the officials go *under the hood* to review a disputed play, but still get the call wrong. They also are tasked with holding both arms in the air, signaling a touchdown when a player is clearly downed on the one yard line.

Referees are also required to punish various types of personal fouls, usually involving one form or another of attack on the ball carrier by an overzealous defensive player. For example, disparaging a running back's barber is a serious penalty resulting in fifteen yards and loss of down.

The Announcers

There are two primary announcers at every game. One is always a former player. He is deemed an expert and loudly questions why something was done instead of something else, by someone else, after each play.

He loudly and regularly reminds the viewers how he would have done it differently during his one year reign as a backup wide receiver on a team that almost made the playoffs.

The other announcer is always a benched regional news broadcaster who still has time remaining on his current employment contract with the Network.

This individual knows nothing whatsoever about the game, but feels compelled to say that one or more of the players is "the best he has ever seen at the position" each time the ball is put into play.

The Head Coach

Coaches receive high level training in scowling, referee baiting, wildly waving their arms while racing up and down the sideline, and clipboard throwing.

They are also skilled in hiding their mouths while a new play is being called, just in case the other team has hired a lip reader who understands what Z21leftomaha might mean.

All coaches have perfected throwing out the red flag to dispute a call on the one play the referees have actually called correctly. The best coaches always follow up by pulling off their head phones and storming out onto the field in feigned disbelief when the penalty doesn't get overturned.

Occasionally the coach will actually call a play, usually resulting in the loss of five yards.

Cheerleaders

There are generally between one and two hundred young athletic women on the sidelines at every game, dressed in what appear to be modified swim suits or underwear.

Their purpose is apparently to distract the other team's players from the game just long enough to cause pass interference (which won't be called), and to encourage the male fans in the stands to buy more beer.

Occasionally, the phrase "deeefense" is delivered, but we're not sure about the reason.

The Kickers

Apparently, during the evolution of American football, someone really dropped the ball and awkwardly left in a minor component of the game that actually involves feet. Each team has two kickers on staff.

The Field Goal Specialist is tasked with either hitting the uprights, veering wide left, veering wide right, or missing the ball completely when attempting a three point score. Of course, not all of this is his fault, due to the fact that the coach is the one who has decided to try the field goal from the fifty yard line instead of going for the six inches needed for a first down. Then, on the next kickoff, the kicker must boot the ball either out of bounds or, if it happens to be an onside attempt, shank it just shy of the required ten yards after hitting the head of one of the offensive linemen.

The Punter is entrusted, on fourth down, to kick the ball as close as possible to the opponent's goal line. In most cases he punches the ball fifteen yards in the wrong direction, falls down, feigning injury due to being run into by a defensive player, and is awarded a first down.

Half Time

Usually, on the same day that the game starts there is a half time. This always consists of an hour or two of commercials, briefly interrupted by analysts in pink or purple ties, back at the studio, advising at length why the team that should be winning isn't.

They confirm this by utilizing complex graphs with arrows and other various markings that are overlaid with brightly colored, computer generated circles on a huge screen. They also argue about why the losing quarterback wasn't forced to retire years ago.

The Red Zone

The red zone is not actually red. It is the place near the opponent's goal line where all teams go for it on fourth down and one, instead of kicking the easy field goal, and fail every time.

The End of the Game

When the two minute warning sounds, you can be certain that the game will possibly end in less than twelve hours, unless there is a tie.

If you are writing a book or building a house during this phase of the commercial time, as previously advised, you may want to consider returning to your Lazy Boy.

Eventually the game ends.

And there you have the basics. For those of you interested in more detailed information regarding football please check out our other series created especially for Boomers titled *Pre-Season: What the Hell?*

Part 4

Legacy

The Grandkids

27

Early Onset Grandparent Syndrome

The beach was warm. The drinks were cool. Umbrellas were required, but only in the drinks.

Dolphins frolicked just off shore, flanked by fishing pelicans. Iguanas and "discount" silver hawkers patrolled the beautiful white sand paradise. Only the hawkers were considered dangerous to humans. They were just coming into season.

The sun was setting over the sparkling blue ocean, and the attendant hovering nearby hurried to our side after he had noticed one of the tequila laced cocktails was getting alarmingly low.

"It is nearly dinner time my friends. Do you wish the double lobster tails again? Or maybe the filet mignon with truffles this time?" he queried. Life was wonderful.

Just then my cell phone rang. I had meant to turn if off while we were at the beach, but my wife insisted on being available, just in case. And sure enough, just in case happened in a big way.

"Hi Dad, it's me," said one of my daughters. The older one I think. The one who had recently gotten married. "Guess what?"

"Ummm - not sure honey," I responded. "Are you still married? I never liked that guy anyway."

"Of course I am, silly," she shot back. "In fact...we're pregnant! Twins!"

My life flashed before my eyes. My vision darkened as I careened off the fluffy lounger onto the warm sand. My drink flew into the air and its colorful umbrella embedded itself in the cushion dangerously close to my foot.

"Too young! Far too young! I'm too young to be a grandpa!" I remembered shouting as the world swirled and blackness efficiently won the battle.

Shortly thereafter I awakened at the airport to the sound of my wife saying to the TSA agent, "Yes, he bought the silver. No, he didn't think he needed a receipt. Yes, that is his fresh guava...what's a strip search?"

Several hours later I gingerly wheeled my now half empty suit case toward the boarding gate. "I think they put your pants back on you inside out," mused my wife.

Eventually, the plane lifted gracefully into the air heading back to our home where the temperature hovered around thirty degrees.

Somewhere in the distance, on the beach below, my filet mignon with truffles was getting cold on the plate. An iguana and a hawker both eyed the meal hungrily.

The official Boomer description for my condition is known as the Terminally Disruptive Early Onset Grandparenting Obligation Syndrome (or TDEOGPOS for short).

It has since been pointed out to us that we apparently are not the only ones who have contracted this insidious and disruptive disease, but that fact has provided small comfort.

Medical science continues to labor for a cure, but to this

point there sadly is none that is effective at any meaningful level. However, we have learned that some of the symptoms can be alleviated if enough funds are available for the treatment.

In truth there are many positives tied to being grandparents. And these of course will be discussed in depth shortly.

First though, let's talk about some of the lifestyle changing scenarios that accompany your evolving Boomer future and oncoming grandparenthood:

- The kids moving back in was always a possibility. Of course it happens immediately.

- Money. Yes, your kid understandably decided to quit her job to take care of the baby, and her husband said he was going to really try to get a paying gig at some point…but could we…

- Hanging out with the grandkids takes on a whole new meaning, usually involving a phrase such as "only for a couple of weeks while we go on a quick trip to the beach for some double lobster."

- You learn that assembling easy to assemble baby related household objects and toys isn't easy. We eventually bit the bullet and bought the Craftsman five hundred piece professional BMW mechanic's tool chest to put together the baby crib with its four thousand parts. Ironically, we never did get it assembled, but we can now competently repair a BMW.

- Diapers and potty training. You are unanimously nominated to handle the night-shift-try-to-hold-it stage.

- Gifting takes on a whole new meaning. For example, apparently the only stroller that will work is the J8500 Custom, priced at thirty-five hundred dollars due to its track tested suspension, six cup holders, and flat screen TV.

- Being on call, in practice, only happens between the hours of two and four AM. This always involves getting something from a store that is thirty or more miles away, which is invariably closed when you get there.

- Feeding time. You are regularly requested to pick up just a few things at the local market, including baby formula (which costs more per ounce that gold dust), natural baby foods (which cost more per jar than the baby formula), and Skittles.

- Holidays always happen at your house, with all the clan. "Ham, turkey, and prime rib again please, and maybe some filet mignon and lobster" for twenty.

- The mall. You are regularly asked to accompany the new mom on a trip to the mall to watch the kids while she does a little shopping. This always results in a six hour stint at the giant rubber boat toy, a fifty dollar lunch bill at the clown restaurant in the food court, and that unfortunate rubber boat cleaning bill.

The most important moment of all for the budding grandparents is learning what the new parents have decided to affectionately call you. Will it be Granny, Gramps, Nana, Papa, or one of a thousand different wonderful variations on the naming of the grandparents?

The actual names selected in your case turn out to have something to do with an apparently famous hip-hop song featuring various body parts and twerking. But after your lawsuit and resulting court order, the family has reluctantly agreed to call you simply Grandma and Grandpa. It is apparently being appealed.

Grandchildren are precious, of course. They are our legacy. And the slight exaggerations noted here in no way take away from the fact that the lion's share of child raising falls on the shoulders of the actual parents. We get that.

But you've heard the phrase "It takes a village." In practice, it actually takes a grandma and grandpa. And in the end, we are pleased and proud to hold those titles.

Now, if we could only find time for some steak and truffles and lobster somewhere warm and far away just for a little while...

28

The Pinewood Derby

Thousands of onlookers cheered as the teams made their way up the steep slope of the great pyramid. The Pharaoh was in attendance, surrounded by an army of priests and warriors.

The contestants had gathered for The Race of the Gods. It had been held each year at this particular location since the time that the Pharaoh's pride, the largest of the pyramids, was built.

Although the huge sloping triangular temples were utilized when a Pharaoh died and was seeking the proper path to the afterlife, they had originally been built for this one specific purpose...The Race.

Each year temple priests, high ranking military commanders, wealthy merchants, and even the Pharaoh himself would work with his eldest son to design and build a small chariot replica.

The idea was that this was the primary passage into adulthood for boys of the aristocracy. It was a divine honor in which the contestant would be required to complete all of the significant tasks and labors of the project himself, with only support and guidance being offered by the father, any other family member, or even friends.

It was not to be about *the winning*, but about the task itself. Although in truth, the winners did receive great riches resulting from their corporate sponsors.

Those who did not follow the required guidelines were to be dealt with harshly.

The race was about to begin.

Hieroglyphs found near Cairo have indicated that a long list of rules and requirements were developed and designed to ensure that Pineset, the God of small wheeled racing structures and periodontal health, was placated through the process of building the divine models.

A large papyrus was later discovered outlining several hundred regulations that the participants were to follow to ensure that no individual would have any unfair advantage in the design and construction of the Chariette (as in small chariot, I surmise). These included:

- Only official materials purchased from what translates as Pharaoh Mart may be used and acquired at The Price (as the hieroglyph tied to topics involving fools and easy marks confirms).

- Each entry must be exactly one quarter cubit by one full cubit and must weigh exactly one third of a stone, not more nor less, lest the offender be plagued with what scholars have translated as everlasting hemorrhoids.

- The racing unit must be designed and built by the child alone. Others may only advise.

The rest of the story is lost to history except for a small engraving found on a stone near a known racing hill with the comment, "and the perpetrators of the infractions were delivered unto Pineset." But I digress.

"Grandpa, do you think a chainsaw would work to shape my car?" quizzed my grandson.

He was of course preparing for the major annual Cub Scout event marketed as the Pinewood Derby, or the I Swear My Kid Built it all by Himself Tournament, as many have come to call it.

After many long days and nights of preparation in which our young racer learned a significant library of new, helpful, and colorful phrases and hand gestures, he was ready. When the big day arrived, our Scout's entry was both shiny and ramp worthy.

The obligatory R2D2 action figure was securely fastened behind the Lego Luke Skywalker on the brightly painted wooden land cruiser. Flame decals were pervasive, as were the washers duct taped with precision behind the plastic wheels. They were perfectly balanced so that the weight of exactly 4.95 ounces was achieved...just under the legal limit of five ounces.

It was in fact, magnificent.

The reason I know that five ounces is the weight limit is not because of the many hours that family members, our hired mechanical engineering and applied physics staff from the university, and our team of lawyers studied the hundreds of pages of rules in the official rule book. (Just kidding).

It is because our neighbor's kid, now a former Cub Scout from a different troop, had made the fatal error the previous week of allowing his vehicle to weigh 5.2 ounces, eliminating him from the derby.

But more on this later.

The Derby was about to begin. The thirty entries were lined up in military precision on the church basement lunchroom stage. The three lane, ramped racing track lurked yellow in the middle of the room, surrounded by dozens of eager and anxious racers and their racing teams. Many of them were in full custom logo printed coveralls carrying clipboards, stop watches, and binoculars.

Finally, the troop leader held up two fingers and stared at the crowd. I later learned that this meant for everyone to be quiet, and was not an affirmation for love and peace, as only Boomers will remember.

Over the next two and a half hours he explained some of the more important derby rules and regulations, and then the racing began!

It is mostly a blur to me now, but know that every flame decaled, graphite balanced, Teflon encased car was allowed to race in each of the three lanes to ensure that there could be no unfair advantage because of conditional racing lane discrepancies.

Ultimately a winner was announced with great fanfare. A large trophy was awarded, and the winner was hoisted by his coverall clad racing team to their shoulders. The sun glistened off his perfect vehicle. Papers were signed, the engineers and lawyers hugged, and all was well.

As an important footnote, our Scout, like his sadly disqualified friend, had actually done most of the construction work on his car himself. He was clearly one of the few in attendance who was able to be truthful when the leader asked about who did the work. We can't prove this of course, but because of the fact that most of the other teams were sponsored by beer and sports shoe companies, we suspected.

In fact, it took a great deal of soul searching to restrain ourselves from moving beyond the advisory role, but we let him create his own masterpiece, except for the purchase of the two hundred dollar ball bearings, the titanium screw assemblies, and the Fermi Lab qualified digital scale, of course.

And in the end our grandson could not have been more proud of the work he accomplished.

Thankfully, there was also an award for most creative unit. And in this regard, our grandson proudly took third place in the robot action figure category.

His two inch trophy now rests on the mantle for future generations of Pinewood enthusiasts to enjoy. Not at all bad for a nine year old who actually built his own car.

Pineset, the ancient mythical Egyptian God, would have been proud.

29

An Ode to Black Friday

It was there in the distance
While I waited in the line
Beckoning, fifty inches
A brand worthy of the time

The temperature had fallen
Some couldn't stand the strain
With tears not tied to pollen
They retreated, and in pain

Comfort I would have offered
If not for the simple plan
That one less item proffered
Meant one more in my hand

The price was less than half they said
One could not be deluded
First come first served was now the rule
For the twenty to be included

Some have said that destiny
Is there for those deserving
This night it was my turn, my friend
Although it was unnerving

Almost there and safe it seemed
The pile not all depleted
First come first served was still the rule
For the two left uncompleted

Terry Killinger

Alas the grandest plan of mine
Was just short of a circuit
So close and yet so far it seemed
The last one, someone took it

And so I bought the next best thing
A brand at twice the price
A name with H and O's and E's
Would do, and would suffice

Since at the store already
More things then did I buy
Black Friday was a great success
But I can't remember why

30

Let There Be Light

The world looked different hanging here upside down from one of the higher gutters. There was the array of twinkling lights in the neighborhood as far the eye could see, as you would expect. You could see that the grass still needed mowing, even at this time of year, but it would have to wait.

It is unclear exactly how I got myself into this tenuous position, although a few things are now coming back to me.

I remember swearing to the entire family, in writing, that I would never ever put up Christmas lights again, even if it meant having to move alone to Greenland or Antarctica...whichever had fewer polar bears.

I remember telling everyone that the five hundred or so dollars that it would cost to hire someone to hang the lights would be well worth it.

I even remember trying to convince the family that leaving last year's lights up - well, forever - would make perfect sense. And that when they were turned off, no one would even notice the oversized, faceted, brightly colored bulbs, particularly late at night. But apparently that idea was deemed tacky.

The wind had picked up a bit, and I had begun twisting in it, so to speak. No one had yet noticed my predicament.

The tweenaged grandson who had enthusiastically

agreed to help put up the lights was standing a few yards away. He was looking in the front window at some game show on the television.

He had been keenly interested in hanging the lights at the top of the gables, even though our ladder was not quite high enough to reach that area.

"Just push me up with a stick after I step on the top rung," he cheerfully suggested. "Wrap the strands of lights around my ankles so that I can use both hands when I get up there."

However, after much discussion, the idea was eventually vetoed by our daughter, although I had presented a strong case in favor, complete with hand gestures, chin rubbing, and the notion that it was common practice in other countries.

That scenario was just a distant memory now. The grandson did indeed help with the process for a while. The first five minutes were, in fact, fantastic.

He was up and down that ladder like a pro. He peeled back the corners of the shingles with remarkable strength, exposing the previously secure waterproofing under layer to the elements for the first time with gusto.

In fact, the first few thousand lights were in place relatively quickly.

Hanging here, upon reflection, it probably would have made a bit more sense to have checked the lights before we put them up, because when we plugged them in - well, you know - nothing happened.

After removing all of the lights from the roof, alone of course, I conducted the belated two hour lighting test.

My assistant, who had previously agreed to help with the bulb checking process, was nowhere in sight.

There he was inside the house, in front of the television, holding what I have been told is called an X-Brick paddle.

He was furiously waving his fists at some sort of demon-like object on the screen. Large letters on the moving image announced:

Welcome to level 196 Ninja Master!

I had replaced and nearly finished installing the now functional lights, when the ladder finally failed.

The sky was beginning to darken. The unfortunate news was that the strand of lights from which I was hanging was beginning to stretch and fail as well.

I could read Made in Trinidad and Tobacco on a small tag near the outlet plug clenched between my teeth. We got them on sale.

The ground looked quite far away from up here, although being upside down helped a bit with the illusion that it wasn't really very high.

In the distance I could hear the fire truck sirens. Clearly someone had finally noticed my situation.

"Hey Grandpa," intoned my legacy. "How the heck did you manage to get your leg stuck in the chimney?"

The second part of that brief conversation was almost unable to be heard due to the fact that he was already back in the living room inspecting some kind of rubber dinosaur, and that my hearing and vision were dimming due to blood loss and the wires tangled around my knee caps.

In time, the fire trucks, ambulance, police department, news crew, hundreds of onlookers, food trucks, and a contingent of political activists appeared in our front yard.

"Hello Dave," shouted the fire chief. "Good to see you again. How's the family this year?"

And I would have cheerfully responded like I did last time, if all those stars in front of my eyes would have stopped flashing for just a moment.

By the way, the lights looked great. And just in the nick of time as well. September was soon going to be upon us and we needed to turn our attention to putting up the tree.

To help others potentially avoid a few of the issues that we have encountered over the years regarding getting ready for the holidays, here are a few ideas that you may find helpful:

Christmas Holiday Preparation Basics

- Acquire some grandchildren. Amazon is a good place to start for this task. Select only ones who are old enough to appreciate the resale value of their gifts, and who have been specifically trained to comment enthusiastically about all the effort and time and money that you have expended on their behalf.

- Buy a Christmas tree. Live ones are best. We usually buy ours in June when they are less expensive. If you live in an area without any live trees, build one from a kit (see Amazon above). Like the lights, the ones made in Trinidad are the best value.

- Begin assembling your ornament ensemble. We usually start with a theme such as rare or extinct deep sea creatures or left handed farming implements. This of course is a full time and ongoing process for the conscientious collector. If you pay less than one hundred dollars per ornament you are doing it wrong. Remember to store your collection in a safe place such as in the garage behind the tire irons and anvils.

- Outdoor lighting is essential. When properly installed there should be no area of your property that is not lit by a colored bulb, including under the house. We often indulge in renting a few electric sub-stations and wind farms to power some of the lighting. Yes, we know that this will not be enough, but it is a good start.

- Begin purchasing your gifts. We always begin with this critical process on December 26th. Remember, heavier is always better, bigger is always bigger, and the more it costs the more love you have to share.

- Think about the things that you will need for the all-important Christmas dinner. We often raise ostriches and armadillos for this occasion for the main course. Blowfish are also always a welcome treat.

- Select your obligatory Santa snack to be placed in front of the fireplace. We have learned that he prefers Scotch, Bourbon, or Jagermeister in the magnum sized (or larger) bottles. Cookies are optional, and he is allergic to milk.

- Prepare your Christmas card list and annual family update letter. We usually purchase pre-written family letters featuring stock pictures of former sitcom actors dressed as elves. This year our family "went" to Europe to see the Alps. We presume that it was fun.

- Have a Christmas party. Be sure to include a visit from Santa. We understand that some of the marginally sober ones who might actually show up can be hired for only a few hundred dollars, if you have an open bar.

- On Christmas Eve at 2:00 AM, when the little ones are presumably sound asleep (they aren't), back the rented twenty eight foot U-Haul up to your front door and begin unloading the dozens of heavy, large, expensive, and unique presents. Hopefully you have used Harry Potter's Dursley family as your model, and are thus well prepared for this important final step. Christmas has arrived.

Or as an extreme last resort, snuggle around the tree in front of a large fire in your pajamas with your family. Open your few personal gifts and sing carols. Later, drink some hot cocoa and enjoy the time of year, the reason for the occasion, and each other's company.

It is just an idea.

31

Some Assembly Required

Christmas Eve had come and gone. It was two in the morning and the kids and grandkids were finally asleep.

The cookies and milk for Santa were in place, and there was even a bowl of uncooked oatmeal laced with cake sprinkles dubbed magic reindeer food. All was well with the world at that moment, except for the one thing.

As retired Boomers, we had made the fatal error of deciding to stay with the family for Christmas, and even worse, agreeing to help.

Loud, peaceful sounding snores could be heard from the master bedroom as our sleeping daughter and her husband dreamed peacefully on into the night.

At some point we had apparently agreed to assemble the fancy new bike that had previously been purchased and was safely hidden in the basement.

It was time. The huge box under the stairs beckoned. After several false starts and painful encounters with floor joists, the star of this year's Christmas show was finally extracted.

The carton itself looked okay, except for the water stains, crushed areas, and some smudging on the bright orange *allow twelve hours for assembly* and *do not swallow parts* labels.

In my estimation the box weighed over two hundred pounds and was six feet wide by twelve feet long.

However, the few words of English on the carton claimed it was only sixty pounds, but surely that was before the packing.

We dragged it upstairs and unpacked it in the family room. At first, it appeared to me that they had forgotten to include instructions. Parts covered every square inch of the room, but no instructions. Finally my wife found them taped to the bottom of the bike seat behind the springs.

Let's see, Spanish, French, Japanese, and some language with only pictures of birds, but no English. However, there were dozens of pages of complex drawings with a multitude of dotted lines showing bolts and washers going into a structure of some kind.

Initially, there was a bit of concern because the required lengthy tool list included pictures of a table saw, jack hammer, fork lift, and bar bells.

There was another image showing something with radioactive symbols next to an outline of a person lying on the ground, highlighted behind a red circle with a bar through it, but - no English.

After an extended period of heavy drinking and contemplation we remembered that this is the new millennium, and that Al Gore had designed the internet for just this moment.

After a long session of Googling, Twittering, and Facebooking (I presume, not fully understanding the entire online process) my wife emerged from the home office, laptop in tow.

"That wasn't so bad, except for that unexpected encounter with a porn site that has the same name as the bike company," she reported.

"And the assembly instructions only cost $299 for the English version - plus shipping and handling, of course."

With the computer precariously teetering on a chair the work was finally under way, with the sun beginning to rise in the East.

We scrolled to the instruction page:

Step 1 - Purchase person to count and review parts precluded in box of happiness (for the moment, the wheels appeared to be missing, but everything else was fine).

Step 2 - Handle bars to frame be attached with importantly. Table saw and fork lift needing is for this step.

Step 3 - Part 689 tinkered extra to part 1023 every time. Noting to person purchase warranty voiding be must if radioactive occurring leak is happen.

In all, there were several thousand steps to the process. When we were done there were many unused parts left on the floor, only a few of which appeared to be important. One of them looked a bit like a seat.

However, we declared the project complete. There was toasting, a small ceremony with candles, and the high-fives and accolades flowed freely. Finally, we proudly placed the completed bike next to the tree.

Christmas morning arrived moments later with a shout of "Santa" from our growing grandson.

He immediately rushed past the shiny new bicycle and

the dozens of other brightly wrapped packages and climbed into the large crushed box leaning against the family room wall. Oil and spilled bourbon stained the back of his pajamas as he shouted, "Can't see me Grandma and Grandpa! Hiding!"

The rest of Christmas day went well in general. After a great breakfast the family went out into the cul-de-sac to begin the process of teaching our grandson how to ride the bike.

We thoughtfully stayed in the house, although loud shouting and swearing could be heard on a disturbingly regular basis outside the front room window.

Eventually, the family came back inside with the father awkwardly holding what looked like a bike seat.

"I ride bike! Broken!" commented our grandson as he climbed back into the packing box.

After retrieving what remained of the bike from the gully behind the house, and applying the needed repairs to the wheels, frame, handle bars, and brakes, we had a great dinner with the family.

As we were driving away, we observed that the seat had gone missing again, and promised to look for it - someday.

The good news is that our family has stopped asking for help of any kind from us on holidays. We're not sure why.

32

The Day Trip

This wasn't going to be easy. We were miles from home, and more than eight thousand feet up in the mountains. Driving the narrow roadway leading up toward the glacier in the National Park seemed like the right thing to do at the time, but now not so much.

We had reached a point on the forest service road where it was no longer possible to turn around. It was late spring, but at this altitude snow was still covering the ground.

In fact, the only way we knew that we were still on the right path was the single set of tire tracks, created by another vehicle, that snaked up the side of the mountain before us. It was probably the ranger who was actually paid to drive on these kinds of roads on purpose, looking for people like us.

A sign in the distance read Glacier Views Ahead, complete with a small picture of a camera. Snow covered the sign post up to the bottom of the sign itself. We could see the tracks continuing past the sign and on up around a dangerous looking bend.

It probably should be mentioned that the grandkids were in the back seat. They had been patient enough to this point, but now were getting a bit wiggly.

We had prepared well in advance for this day trip, of course, socking in multiple snacks spanning the sweet/sour/soft/hard/chewy ranges. There were movies on the tablet, board games, a full tennis court, and swimming pool.

At this exact moment my young granddaughter declared, "I need to go to the bathroom!"

This concept was not on my original list of trip preparation topics, nor part of the grand day trip plan at any level. I suppose it should have been, and at the moment, the thought that it may have become an issue crossed my mind.

"Can you hold it?" I posed.

"Got to go! Now!" my granddaughter responded helpfully. Then it started to snow - hard. We finally pulled over and Grandma helped with the situation. It wasn't pretty.

Now, we like snow. Who doesn't? But at the moment it made things a bit inconvenient.

We could see flashing lights up ahead just past the glacier sign. A vehicle of some type was headed back down the hill toward our car. We had become quickly snowbound in an area in which there was no turn-around (as previously mentioned), and we were grateful for the impending rescue.

"Look Grandpa, a bear!" mentioned our grandson. Sure enough, a large brown bear and her two cubs had run out of the woods and set up camp on our front bumper.

"I really need to go again. Bad." suggested our granddaughter. The flashing red and blue lights were now shining brightly just in front of our car.

"You in the car! Stop interacting with those bears immediately! You don't have any food in the car do you?" a disembodied voice crackled over a loudspeaker of some sort.

My grandson stopped chewing on his Twix bar, chocolate pasting all corners of his face, and looked up. The ice chest full of beef snacks and salmon, strapped to the roof, was being pawed at by the mother bear.

Fortunately, the ranger had apparently faced this sort of situation in the past. He honked the horn on his four wheel drive and flashed his headlights. The bears, clearly startled, quickly finished shredding our cooler, and ambled back into the woods.

The baby bears frolicked in the snow, tumbling over and over while eating the remains of our gourmet cheesecake, and drinking our juice flavored energy drinks and bourbon. It was quite amusing to see them having trouble inserting the little straws into the drink boxes.

Soon they were gone from sight.

The ranger approached our car, flashlight in hand. He did not look pleased. He reached the driver's side window and motioned for me to open it.

Shortly thereafter, we were being towed off the mountain, bear feeding citation in hand. My granddaughter intoned, "Never mind Grandpa. Don't need to pee anymore."

The rest of the day trip was uneventful.

Tips for Avoiding Your Next Day Trip

- **Feign Illness** - This is one of our favorites. Grandparents get sick all the time. Be sure to include the phrase "highly contagious."

- **The Car Won't Start** - Once again, foolproof unless your son or daughter advises, "Just use my car." In this case you always can try launching the idea that "we aren't comfortable..." However, that never works.

- **Weather** - Too hot -Too cold - Too humid - Pending storm (distance from your state not important). You get the idea.

- **Cramps/Pulls/Joints** - Boomers get these things all the time. Grab your side and bend over for best effect.

- **Big Game on Television** - Soccer is best for this strategy. No one ever really knows when these games are being played or what the teams are actually doing during the game. Say you are rooting for the orange team.

- **Incontinence/Bloating/Vision Problems** - see cramps above.

- **Leave the County/State/Country** - in the night.

- **Palpitations** - Highly effective, as long as you don't over offer what exactly is palpitating.

- **Pending Meteor Showers** - One could happen. You never know.

- **Catastrophic Mobile Phone/Internet/Texting Failure** - Scripting suggestion: "Oh, did you try to call? Did you try texting? Must be a dead zone."

Every Boomer is different. The specific strategies and tactics you use to attempt avoiding the day trip request, and subsequently being locked up in a small, enclosed space (your car), for up to twelve hours with colicky grandchildren, are endless.

Of course, none of them ever really work for long, and presently you will be headed off toward some lake, mountain, desert, former nuclear waste site, or even worse, a mall.

And if we can make just one final suggestion - make them pee before you leave. However, that will make no difference ten minutes after you are on the road.

Enjoy!

33

The One That Got Away

They were not supposed to be in this part of the ocean. The navigational maps on the bridge all had the same large red marks on them, outlining this particular area as fatally off limits. Still the massive vessel proceeded at flank speed into the forbidden zone.

The captain had prepared well, or so he kept telling himself as he looked out through his binoculars to the horizon from the bridge of the monstrous whaling ship.

Something did not look right with the sky, and even less so with the sea. Naturally, to complicate matters, the wind had picked up and the temperature had dropped several degrees in the last few minutes. Dark clouds were beginning to form to starboard, sporting an unmistakable swirl. Waves began to throw huge plumes of spray over the bow. The first mate looked up from the radar screen with a stricken look in his eye and shook his head.

For the first time the captain briefly questioned his obsession with the quest he had dreamed about his whole life.

It had begun one morning long ago while reading about his current quarry on the back of a Fruity Pebbles cereal box. The article's heading described Mythological Beasts of the Ocean featuring The Mighty Kraken - God of the Sea. It was why he had become a sea captain.

He had studied books, testimonials, ship's logs, charts, and a long list of speculative theories about the existence and location of the beast, and concluded it was not mythology. It was real!

The location of the hunt was just off the coast of Bermuda, in an area that formed a crude triangle on the charts.

In the early days, scientists occasionally dropped sensors to study the lava vents that snaked along the bottom in this region, miles below the surface. But the technology wasn't really up to the task.

Then the deep sea probes had begun. Only a few at first, but then it seemed they were everywhere. Their impossibly bright lights punched into the murky depths, finally one day shining into the eyes of the Kraken itself.

What is this? it pondered, and then quickly took action. All of the probes after that were lost - crushed - presumably due to the extreme water pressure at this great depth. The Kraken chewed on the latest set of remains thoughtfully. *Needs salt.*

It wasn't long until the beast swam up from the depths for the first time. Ultimately, it breached the surface not too far from a passing ship. Poetically, the vessel was manned by a miserable gang of pirates out of the Azores, who had just ravaged and sunk a large pleasure boat.

Uncertain of the nature of the object, the Kraken lashed out, and in one swipe crushed the ship and its crew. There was only one survivor besides the tiny poodle that continued to bark relentlessly aboard the remains of the pirated pleasure craft. It was the first mate from the pirate vessel that was sinking quickly nearby.

The first mate paddled over to the wildly barking dog and attempted to coax it on to the makeshift raft to which the pirate was lashed. The dog just growled, and then clamped onto the marauder's leg with some very sharp teeth, foam covering the corners of the dog's mouth.

They floated for days on a mass of debris, and eventually washed up on a beach in the Bahamas. No one believed the fanciful tale about a monstrous beast taking down the vessel. Ironically, the pirate died a few weeks later, apparently from rabies, and the story died along with him.

Over the years, there were other ships, and even planes, lost in the area. Eventually the incidents diminished. The Kraken had returned to its warm home in the depths, until today.

Yes, the moment had arrived. The captain was finally hunting the Kraken. Nothing else mattered now. Nothing was going to get in his way. Nothing.

The sonar signaled a hit. Slowly, from the edge of the newly cracked radar screen, a green mass began to emerge as the needle oscillated back and forth. The scale of the image was not to be believed.

The crew was tightly gripping any available handhold to stay upright as the mate shouted, "Turn back now Captain! Turn back now!" But the captain was nowhere in sight on the bridge.

He had made his way up to the gigantic harpoon cannon at the fore of the ship. There he stood, awaiting his nemesis like a modern day Captain Ahab. *It's not the same*, he thought to himself as another wave washed over his position. *This time it will be different.*

The Kraken slowly rose from the depths. This particular

part of the ocean was famous for its depths. In fact, the creature had spent most of its near immortal life near the volcanic vents. The funnels billowed superheated debris at nearly a thousand degrees Fahrenheit. *Nice and warm*, thought the beast.

The captain saw the water boil wildly in front of the ship. Huge tentacles of an impossible size thrashed into the sky before him. A massive eye appeared above the waves and quickly focused on the ship, and more specifically on the captain manning the harpoon.

Food, thought the Kraken.

After waiting his whole life for this moment, the captain took his shot. He watched, as if in slow motion, the harpoon miss its mark by a wide margin. A few minutes later the stern of the former whaling ship slipped beneath the waves for the last time, as the captain shook an angry fist at the sky.

Tasty, mused the beast. *Need to cut back - been eating more now that I am pregnant.* The hideous monster slowly descended to its home miles below the surface.

"That's quite a story you've been telling there, son," commented the Boomer aged fisherman sitting on the dock at the pond with his twelve year old grandson. "How the heck do you even know what a Kraken is?"

"Bart Simpson got eaten by one. Twice!" stated the boy, having finally finished his long tale. "Wait! I got a bite!" The six inch Crappie that had already been hooked and reeled in several times experienced another presumably uncomfortable catch and release moment.

The fishing continued.

Fishing is a critical step in the successful development of all pre-teens and evolving Boomers.

Most parents are too smart to waste their time sitting on the bank of a mosquito infested pond for several hours, watching others nearby limit out while they catch nothing.

The grandparents are therefore always entrusted with the sacred role of gutting and scaling on the rare occasion that a keeper is caught.

The fishing process involves a complex ritual requiring many steps and key equipment acquisitions to work properly.

Here are some of the concepts and planning you will need to complete before taking that first fateful trip to the pond with your young fisherperson:

Equipment Basics

Unlike many sports, fishing doesn't need to cost a lot to get started. With that in mind however, don't forget that the grandkid is your pride and joy, in fact your legacy, we might say.

Your equipment options are:

- The Basics

    or

- Recommended (for those grandchildren you love)

Equipment Options

Basic	Recommended
Pole	
Wal-Mart Fiberglass Kit $22.95	Aircraft Grade Titanium *Ninja* Hand Painted $1950
Reel	
Wal-Mart Quick Release (included with pole)	*Bass-Tech* Cast-Master Platinum Model $2700
Tackle Box	
Target Brand 12" $9.95	*Peyton Manning* Branded Guppy-Buddy $495
Fishing Tackle	
Target Brand Starter Assortment $9.95	*Martha Stuart* Big-Bobber Tackle Assortment $395
Bait	
Worms (from Garden) $0	*Guy Fieri* Baby Squid and Frog Mix $440
Boat	
None	*Bayliner* 22' Barracuda-Buster $37,900
Total Investment	
$42.85	$43,880

What to Wear

There are several different schools of thought about what a fisherperson should wear at the lake or stream.

While there is general consensus that a sweat shirt, jeans, some kind of light weight jacket, and hip waders are always a good choice, opinions diverge wildly on the subject of hats.

Many fishing pros prefer the outback style cap, while others deem the boater's hat the best choice. It is a matter of which one makes you look more ridiculous.

The key is to always put a wide assortment of lures, dozens of brightly colored flies, and plenty of rubbery looking purple or green worm-like attachments on the hat of your choice. Of course, none of the lures or flies on the hat will ever be used in the actual fishing process.

Often, the best fisherpeople add creative text to the hat as well. One of our favorites is *I'm already over my limit*, but it is completely up to you.

Clearly, it is important to select the proper attire to make it look like you have actually been fishing before at some point in your life. The fact that you once fainted while inadvertently seeing the fish monger clean a trout at the public market is not important.

About Bait

The concept of selecting the correct bait for your current fishing situation is a rich subject indeed. The fishing aisle at the local Wal-Mart, for example, has over one million choices of lures, flies, and related rubbery and shiny bait related products.

They also have live worms (glow in the dark night crawlers are the most popular), crickets, minnows, squid, and tadpoles in a cooler in the beer and wine section.

The fishing pros also use marshmallows, cheese, bacon, bourbon, and filet mignon as standard bait choices. However, the bourbon and filet mignon options rarely make it onto a hook.

In the end, it is recommended that you just start with worms. They only cost a few dollars each, and are easy to use.

Also, it is completely understood that you personally have no intention of actually baiting your grandkid's hook yourself. Professional hook baiters are easily found on Craig's List for only a hundred dollars an hour. The more troubling issue is that your grandchild shouldn't have named the worms.

Great news! You are now ready to fish!

Where to Fish

Regardless of where you live (except for those of you living in or near Death Valley) there are generally a variety of great fishing holes to visit with that new grand-fisherperson in your family.

Ask the pros at the bait shop for suggestions. They won't tell you, of course, about their current secret hole. They may even direct you to the drain overflow area at the sewage treatment plant instead, but it is a good place to start.

Next, check out all the places that you fished as a kid. Naturally, all of them will now be paved over and developed with high rise condos or pet therapist businesses, completely obscuring that special spot where you once almost caught a bass.

Eventually you will stumble across a public fishing sign, after making a wrong turn again while coming home from happy hour, pointing to a nearby pond.

Let the fishing begin!

The Art and Science of Fishing

You've seen the beautiful shots on the National Geographic Channel of the intrepid fisherperson standing midstream, whipping the line back and forth before landing the fly perfectly in the middle of the best fishing hole in the region, right?

It will be exactly the same for you and your grandkid on your first day at the lake, except you'll be on a semi-submerged former boat dock, with twenty seven other grandparents all trying to catch the same bullhead.

Just remember that it is not the actual number of fish that you take home to the frying pan. It is the experience itself that you are seeking.

Keep thinking this as you untangle the line from the high output power transmission feed again. And it's a good thing you made your grandkid wear a life jacket. He appears to be floating away from the dock at the moment towards a submerged Buick.

You see! Fishing is both an art and a science. The Catfish Channel announcer said it, so it must be true.

That's the basics. There is just one more thing to consider:

Mapping the Nearest Hospital, Police and Fire Stations, and Air Rescue Headquarters

It is just a suggestion.

Fish Stories

In the end, the memories that you will create while fishing with your family will be well worth the price of the equipment, the medical bills, and the bail bonds.

We probably should have mentioned earlier in the discussion that you will need to acquire fishing licenses. It was always a long shot that you would actually catch a fish, however, except for the exact moment the game warden happens by.

Fishing is a rite of passage. It is a bonding experience. It is a great tool for future use as a threat to do it again when your grandkids ask you to buy a puppy.

One day, medical science may find a way to get that brightly colored, feathered fly lure removed from your nose.

In later years, while sitting around the fire at a family reunion (before the fire engines arrive), you will recount to your relatives the greatest moments that you had while fishing with your grandkid, including the tale about the twenty pounder that he reeled in after playing it for six hours, and the full limit trout dinner that you cooked at the edge of the river while being chased by a bear.

And of course about *the one that got away.*

34

Take It from the Top

The ground trembled. At first it seemed that no reasonable explanation would sort out the source of the phenomenon. Animals of every size and type hurtled from their daytime hiding places onto front porches and out into the busy streets. Fear was palpable in their eyes.

Nothing, it seemed, could stand in the way of their retreat as they careened away from the unearthly sounds that emanated from the nearby structure.

The big lake, not too far away, boiled with the incredible emergence of a school of giant squid that had not surfaced for thousands of years, tentacles frantically waving as they swam quickly away from the cacophony.

It was in fact, pick your instrument day at the local school.

"Okay everyone! Let's have your attention up here to the front. Pick another instrument to try," said the teacher.

"Peter, that was a good effort on the tuba, but remember that being the loudest isn't always the best. And all you flute players, don't let the broken glass from the shattered windows bother you. It happens all the time."

"Ready, let's go."

Band

Music teachers will tell you that there should be a law that no one should be allowed to play any instrument until they have mastered it. In the real world, however, this is not always possible.

As a Boomer and a grandparent, you may be approached for input on the subject of selecting that first instrument. Hiding in the woods or behind the dumpster at the mall often helps you avoid this challenge, but eventually you will be found.

Choosing an Instrument

Your son or daughter will approach you one day with the information that your grandchild has been tasked with picking a musical instrument at school. And that it must be chosen and acquired before school begins tomorrow.

The choices will include the flute, trumpet, French horn, clarinet, grand piano, tuba, full drum kit, and the bass piccolo.

Of course, your grandchild will select the grand piano, after having watched a cat play one of them on the internet. It would not be an issue if you actually possessed a grand, or even a not-so-grand version of the instrument. However, a good used Steinway can be obtained for thirty thousand dollars or so.

The grandkid's next choice will certainly be the bass piccolo. And you are fine with this until you learn that they don't make this particular instrument anymore, and that you would have to buy one on eBay if you want to pursue the concept. Base price - thirty thousand dollars.

Sometime just before midnight, after agreeing to buy your grandchild a new car on his sixteenth birthday if he doesn't choose the piano, the piccolo, or the drums, the kid settles on the tuba.

Thankfully one of those can be had for only a couple thousand dollars if you don't mind a few dents and missing parts.

Finally, you and your family ponder the minor detail of acquiring one by nine o'clock the next morning.

Acquiring your Instrument - Part One

Miraculously, Ms. Spratt, the music teacher, has gotten the flu will not be in school the next day. It appears that you have a day or two to handle the situation.

The local music store is located downtown in the middle of a long term construction area. After paying to park in a parking garage a half mile away, you enter the store.

You learn that they did have a great tuba - exactly the one you were looking for - except that someone bought it just a couple of hours ago. However, they are having a big sale on full drum kits, and they have plenty of grand pianos.

You check out eBay and see that someone has a tuba in the right price range in Nova Scotia. Craig's list offers a better selection but you balk at giving out your social security number, home address, shoe size, and bank account numbers before the sellers will tell you the price.

Acquiring your Instrument - Part Two

Unbeknownst to you or your family until this point, your grandchild had previously been given a complete packet of information about the option of renting an instrument. It had somehow found its way into the bottom of his sock drawer a month ago.

Your grandchild offers up this piece of news unsolicited while eating another pudding cup. You read the details about instrument rental from the Usury Brothers Lease Corporation LLC, based in the Balkans.

It turns out that all you need to do is provide your social security number, home address, shoe size, and bank account numbers, along with three copies of your birth certificate, proof of employment, and six personal references for the privilege of renting a dented tuba with missing parts for three hundred dollars a month.

Since you are the only family member with a credit rating high enough to be considered, you reluctantly sign the paperwork. You even sign the form on page twenty six that says that the dented and pock marked instrument was received in perfect condition.

Problem solved.

It is at this point that your grandchild has decided that he would rather play the flute.

Practice Makes Perfect

As part of the Boomer experience, you will often be asked to help with the grandkids' daily practice sessions. This usually occurs in the form of a text message from your son or daughter asking if you would be willing to hang out with the grandkids tomorrow just for a little while and, by the way, they will need to practice.

Your previous attempt with this type of assignment involved retrieving the budding musician from the heavily wooded area down in the gully, with the help of the local police and fire departments.

You reluctantly agree to help. The actual process of

getting your grandchild to practice is really quite simple, and not unlike working through the five stages of grief.

Here are the basic options you will need to consider:

- As a long shot, take the high road at least once, and say "it's time to practice (insert name here)," and see what happens. Pause. We didn't think so.

- Print out a calendar and buy a box of large shiny multicolored stars. Theoretically you will use the gold ones for successful practice sessions, although we all know this will actually never occur. Instead, use the gold stars for sessions in which there are only a few swear words or direct threats to you or your dog's life during the practice period.

    Save the blue and red stars for use in a preselected set of practice violation scenarios including the setting of small fires and destruction of minor family heirlooms.

    Only use the green stars when the instrument or house is damaged or destroyed, preferably no more than twice weekly if possible.

- Tell your grandchild that if they don't practice there will be no television or outside activities during your visit. However, now that they have smart phones, they just don't care.

- In the end, you may want to adopt the standard practice rules and guidelines that most parents and grandparents have used since the beginning of time:

    - Call your child in from the yard.
    - Set a timer for five minutes.

- Tell them they have to practice until the timer goes off.
- The timer goes off.
- Send them back outside.

Performances and Recitals

The time will come when your grandchild will get a pink or canary colored bond paper announcement from their school describing the big Spring Fling music performance in the cafeteria. The document will sport many exclamation points and marketing phrases.

Chances are high that your grandchild's band or orchestra instructor will have chosen the full three hour score of Wagner's Valkyrie for the elementary kids to perform. It is in this situation that all those minutes of practice will have come in handy.

The playing begins. The hundreds of cell phone pictures that you take of your prodigy sitting in the back row, instrument in hand, looking up at a bird that got in through the heat vent, will be precious additions to the family album.

And you've only had to endure the proceedings for an hour. Then the second movement begins.

A World without Music?

Music is a cornerstone of the human condition. Some say it derives from the fundamental biology of the heartbeat, breathing, and other natural body rhythms. Some say it emanates from the invisible movement of atoms and even smaller particles in our universe. In string theory there is even a proposal that the universe itself is comprised of musical waves.

Almost every culture in the world has traditions, rituals, and legends shared through song and dance. Almost every religion relies on music to help connect the divine with the people.

There are songs about love, lost love, hoped for love, tragic love, wronged love, misplaced love, and a thousand other variations. Great composers changed the world with only wooden boxes tied to strings, awkward metal horns, and the human voice as their tools.

We share music at the most critical times in our lives, when we are young, when we find love, when we marry, and when we die.

Whether you or your kin have the gift, getting involved in music at some level will pay dividends in wonderful and unintended ways for all of us.

All kidding aside - May there never be a world without music.

35

Watch This!

The Earth looked magnificent from this height. You could see the continents turning slowing within the curved horizon. You could see the lights of distant cities as they sparkled in the night on the other side of the world. It seemed that you could almost see Heaven.

But then the upward momentum began to wane. It occurred to you that, at this height, it may not be pretty getting back down.

How did this happen anyway?

As an emerging Boomer, just a few minutes ago you were sipping another wine cooler out of your *World's Best Poisonous Reptile Wrangler* mug, the one they tell you was apparently awarded to you sometime during your last trip to Florida.

One minute the grandkids were bouncing away on their new trampoline that Santa had delivered over the holidays, and the next you were up here among the clouds, just beginning a downward arc, and suddenly, seriously considering your future.

Life had been good, you mused. Scenes of past accomplishments and failures flashed before your eyes. The day you proposed to your wife while cliff jumping, the time you thought feeding that grizzly bear cub near its mother was the right thing to do, and the time you won the hot dog eating contest by twenty dogs. All of it flashed before your eyes. It had been a good life.

Then the world tilted once again and you were down. The family rushed onto the platform to check on your condition. You could hear a couple of the grandkids fighting over who would get your stamp collection. Your wife was crouched over you sobbing and looking up the number for 911.

Then you opened your eyes. *Ouch*, you pondered, but nothing seemed broken. Sirens wailed in the distance, getting louder by the minute. *Next time maybe I'll try a flip* was your last thought for several hours.

Trampolines are great fun, they tell me. In the real world I have never really been on one. When the notion was brought up that the grandchildren might be getting one, I gently pushed back on the idea.

"No! No! No! No! Never ever! Don't even think about it! You've got to be flipping idiots!" and a few other helpful suggestions were presented by me at the time.

Of course, the trampoline was acquired the very next day.

Upon reflection, maybe it wasn't such a bad idea after all. In fact, so far there have been no deaths, only a few maimings, and no known loss of limbs. However, we just finished assembling the unit a few minutes ago. Time will tell.

Assembling Your New Trampoline

To say that the box that Santa had left was enormous would be far too weak a description. My estimation was that it wouldn't fit in the rented, full sized moving van. My wife briefly accused me of exaggeration until she saw the box sinking into the eight inch thick concrete driveway.

After all, it had taken three of Santa's helpers at the Big Present Store to get the thing into the van in the first place. It had taken four less hardy helpers to get it back out on Christmas Eve.

Fortunately, we only nearly lost one of our helpers in the process. He became entangled in the plastic strapping and was dragged under the box as it was being excavated. He is however, expected to recover.

Eventually the package was positioned next to the tree and beautifully wrapped in several dozen rolls of gift paper, waiting for Christmas morning to arrive.

After the excitement of the gift opening was finally over, it was time to face into the reality that the trampoline probably wouldn't work very well unless it was taken out of the box and ultimately assembled.

Reluctantly, after drinking heavily and buying more insurance, we opened the box. In the process, we somehow inadvertently released one of the many restraint mechanisms presumably designed to hold the contents in place.

Thousands of small parts launched themselves across our back yard and into the street. The dog grabbed and carried away what appeared to be one of the support legs, but the picture on the carton showed plenty of other legs. Not a big problem.

The instructions were in the bottom of the box. At six hundred pages it was an impressive sight. A large red circle with a bar through it filled the front page of the book, superimposed over a picture of a completed trampoline.

Although the bright red wording below the circle was in

some foreign language, it surely said, *Never use this product for any purpose ever! What were you thinking?* Or something similar.

Pages two through eighty had the same red circles with a variety of red stick people images in various states of distress. The figures with crosses in their eyes and their torsos and legs in different parts of the picture looked particularly disturbing.

It was time to begin construction. Thankfully, one of our helpers knew Swahili and was able to clarify some of the steps.

"Step One: Putting legs and springs into bouncy net importantly working must be," he intoned, pointing at a picture of some parts that vaguely resembled some of the pieces in the box. "Being do this many times and finish bestly with quickness assemble."

Eventually the trampoline was assembled. Yes, there were some missing parts, and other parts were left over. One of the springs was discovered over a mile away embedded in a street sign. And someone pointed out that there probably should have been a net around the structure like it showed in the picture. But in general the thing looked pretty good.

It was time to let the grandkids enjoy the act of hurtling themselves into the air in a series of uncontrolled spring assisted maneuvers. Let the fun begin!

There is more to tell, but in the interest of time, and the various pending lawsuits, let it be said that the project was a complete success.

In fact, one of the neighbors called and said that they had bought one as well, and requested just a little help getting it out of the car.

We moved out that night, without offering a forwarding address.

Trampoline Fun Facts

- Buford Schmidlap, the purported inventor of the modern trampoline in the early eighteen eighties, died young. In fact it happened during the unveiling of his new device in the town square. His last words were reportedly, "Watch this!"

- Sun Tzu, in his famous *Art of War* document stated, "Forfeit bounce demon to enemy feigning regret. Death comes suddenly to all. Victory quickly follows."

- Petroglyphs found in Northern Europe indicate that trampolines may have been used by Neanderthals over fifteen thousand years ago. The images generally show a framework covered by what appears to be dinosaur skin with a stick human figure high above with little crosses in its eyes.

- Trampoline safety guidelines clearly state that only one person at a time may be on the unit, although in real life this only actually happened once. And in that case the one individual jumping slipped and landed on the other jumper waiting his turn at the bottom of the ladder.

- In the French Revolution trampolines were briefly considered as an execution device instead of the guillotine, but quickly dismissed as being too cruel.

- NASA experimented with trampolines in the late

sixties as potential launch vehicles. The tests were quickly abandoned when the capsules were consistently sent too far into space with no practical means of recovery.

- Recently, scientists have identified a DNA indicator tied to an individual's propensity to be attracted to trampolines. However, the trend for this particular evolutionary flaw should soon be eradicated from the gene pool.

- The Chinese word for trampoline, hang gong now, translates to "very bad idea."

- A recent lawsuit charging that a large trampoline manufacturer has been knowingly shipping products constructed with defective and sub-par materials has been dismissed by the Supreme Court. In a rare nine to zero decision the court cited the premise, "What difference would it make?" in their report.

Any time is the right time to acquire that first trampoline. However, they happen to be on sale right now down at the Big Present Store due to the many returns after Christmas. We have heard that some stores actually ended up with more trampolines than they originally sold.

In any case, I have completed the assembly of two functioning trampolines at this point, the second one involving a party bet and a beverage described by the host as Fireball.

In fact, I have applied for my contractor's license and have purchased one of those fancy delivery vans that you see on the television commercials. I'm going to call the company Bouncers! Trampoline Assembly and Medical Supplies.

I still wear the neck brace, of course, and use the crutches. My former wife calls every now and then from somewhere in Florida where she apparently works at a poisonous reptile farm. She said it is a much safer work environment.

Go ahead Boomers. Life is short. Put a little bounce in your step.

36

Did I Do That?

Although it was the middle of the day, the sky was completely black. Clouds of sinister ash spewed for miles into the previously brightly sunlit atmosphere.

Lava, red-orange and horrible, lurched high above the widening cone below. Molten rock, and the trees and houses that it carried, poured down the mountain side and into the town in slow motion.

Visitors and onlookers screamed as they ran to avoid the onslaught. Mothers grabbed their children in their arms as they attempted to escape the encroaching river of death.

"Stand back. It's headed your way!" shouted a balding older man in a leather elbowed sweater. He was the unlikely leader of the rescue team. He waved his arms at the retreating crowd and the growing army of rescue workers.

The fire department, along with every other available rescue resource, was on the scene, but it was a hopeless task. Brave men and women in hazard suits simply stood with their arms folded, powerless to do anything at all to save the day.

Lightning cut the horizon as thunder boomed relentlessly over the growing cone. Hot rain and molten ash covered everything on the ground. The pounding hail took its toll on the multitude of recently purchased BMW's and Land Rovers parked nearby.

"Save the children! Save the score cards!" shouted the diminutive teacher as he ran towards the towel bins at the back of the school gym.

A small, frightened dog barked at the flowing lava outside, but was quickly carried to safety by yet another fearless fire fighter. The black sky appeared to grow even darker as all hope dimmed.

At the rear of the retreating crowd stood a dazed and bewildered sixth grader. His sweater vest was covered with gray ash. His mother and father were racing in his direction shouting for him to run, but he wouldn't leave.

Fortunately, in the distance, the belching monstrosity had stopped growing, and the plumes of debris were beginning to diminish, if only slightly.

Although the volume of the eruption was still deafening, a small voice could be heard nearby...

..."Maybe I used a bit too much baking soda," considered the young bespectacled science fair participant. "I wonder if they will take points off for that?"

Hot ash continued to fall on the stricken town.

The Science Fair

Most Boomers can remember either participating in, or at least going to, a series of science fairs as they grew up. A few of the participants at these fairs actually went on to accomplish great things in science or business.

One member of our graduating class almost made it to the big time. He had invented the Six Hour and Thirty Minute Recharging Elixir, but ultimately his product was beaten to the market by what is now known as the

Five Hour Energy Drink.

In any case, it is common for an unsuspecting parent to receive an unsolicited memo from the elementary or middle school, always on pink or salmon colored copy paper, announcing the next upcoming Spectacular Science Fair Extravaganza.

Missing will be a torn off section of the signup sheet, due to the fact that your son or daughter will have already taken the initiative to enroll.

The inevitable questioning about the tentative topic selection will result in the universal response, "Um...I put down something about the effects of toxic waste on siblings...I think. I can't really remember."

As a Boomer and presumed current grandparent, this type of event will mark the beginning of your long, unintended, life changing sortie into the amazing world of science. There will be others.

It often begins a few hours before a series of critical science fair deadlines are due, while you are in the car on the way to happy hour. The parents of your budding grand-scientist will approach you with an offhand comment such as, "Hi Mom, hi Dad, Theodore's first draft of the science fair presentation is due first thing tomorrow morning. Would you mind stopping by the mall on your way home from the city council meeting that you said you were going to be attending tonight? We just need a few things for the project."

Then, after a very long pause, "Sure," we reluctantly respond.

The convoluted and inevitably debilitating process that then follows is far too complex to document in this simple forum. To be fair about it, we did actually know someone who did not have to ultimately be institutionalized after performing the assigned duties. They now live in a hut in Iceland. However, when it is your turn to participate in a similar event, we are sure that everything will be fine.

Now that the meds are mostly working, we will share a few of the more basic steps that always occur from the parent and grandparent perspective, in the world of science fair preparation and execution.

Just to be clear, in this situation, the word execution has nothing to do with capital punishment - yet.

Important Things to Know About Your Involvement in the Science Fair

- All potential projects will sound great at first to your student. However, none will be just right enough to make the cut, until six minutes before the final topic selection is due.

- The project selected will be the most complex and expensive of the options, and also the most dangerous.

- Of the hundred or more parts needed, all will be readily available at the local Home Depot, except the final few critical components. For example, you will need to use online purchasing for the commonly required jet engine and nuclear reactor.

- The assembly instructions that your scientist will have garnered from the internet, describing how to construct the project, will never be in English. Luckily you already know that African clicking language.

- After all parts are purchased and mostly constructed, your student will change his mind about the project's chances of winning first place, and will advise the *project team* that he wants to start over.

- At this stage of the process you will discover that your home owner's, medical, and dental insurance will have all been cancelled. It will never be clear how they found out about your involvement, but it will too late.

- All parts for the new project will need to be overnighted via FedEx to get them in time for the event. None of the parts for the revised presentation will be available at Home Depot, except for the always important bucket.

- When you arrive back home from the science fair there will be several black SUV's parked in front of your house with Homeland Security marked in small letters on the doors. They will be wanting to talk with you about your successful attempt to buy spent cobalt reactor cores on Craig's List. This may not go well.

- Your student's exhibit will also require a four color ten by ten foot three panel display, which you will acquire from the local printer for three hundred dollars. Your student's name and the project title will be misspelled, but it will be too late for any corrections at this point.

- Tears are to be expected at this stage. The student may also cry a bit as well, but not usually.

- The presentation will go well. However, first place will be awarded to the student who bought the rejected first project from you at ten cents on the dollar. The winning student's picture will be in the regional news, and he will be offered a full ride to Stanford by the school's science department.

- Your student will receive a purple ribbon labeled Participant.

After most of the fires have been put out, the minor electrocutions tended to, and the gerbil bites salved, you can finally rest.

Homeland Security will probably still be at your house, but your lawyers will have advised you that time served is a phrase that may be of significant value in this particular situation.

The first of the credit card bills will have arrived, and thankfully the maximums were met quickly during your science project preparation period. Ironically, all of your purchases will have helpfully raised your credit limit by several thousand dollars.

Your former grand-scientist will have already forgotten about the fair, and will be suggesting to his parents that band camp may be a great idea for the summer.

The soon to be band member will have already selected an instrument that he is certain will cause his current prospective interest to notice him. The instrument selected at the moment will be a privately branded Led Zeppelin full custom drum kit with imported zirconium cymbals.

Rest assured there will be another science fair next year, with the added component of the younger sister participating as well.

You have been advised by your other grandchild that a live hippo exhibit would be great next year. In this regard, the Fish and Wildlife Service and Animal Control already have you in their databases.

Part 5

The Pasture

37

The Art of Getting Old

The sky was the brightest of blues. From up here it felt like you could see forever, all the way to the horizon and beyond.

A flock of geese, far off in the distance, appeared to be heading south for the winter. Ice crystals glistened on their flapping wings, the little ones flying frantically to keep up with the rest of the huge V. It almost seemed as if they were acknowledging your victory by performing a small dip in the formation.

The sun sparkled high in the endless vista.

Your breath came in short bursts as you stood there in triumph. You raised your fist high into the air like that guy did in the boxing movie.

People standing nearby began clapping rhythmically, whistling, and shouting in recognition of your accomplishment. *Hey! That looks like the mayor headed this way to congratulate me,* you contemplated.

"So you made it up the steps again," said my wife. "Thank God there were only six of them."

Getting old is both an art and a science. The fact that you are getting a bit older is not an easy topic to digest. But we are here to help.

Consider the following key categories of your inevitable unraveling:

Meds

We were here at the mall because of the commercial on television. The nice man who looked like a doctor said that there was finally a cure for restless leg syndrome. "Are your legs restless?" asked my wife.

"Well, now that you mention it, I did feel a twinge during our trip to the liquor store when I picked up one of the larger cases," I responded thoughtfully.

"And then there was the time you got that cramp in your foot," she mused. "We need to get us some of that medicine now! It's on sale, too!"

We continued our journey deeper into mall, to the store named Pill Party Plus!

There were brightly colored bottles, cans, and boxes stacked high as far as the eye could see, which wasn't very far at this point in our lives.

Loud, auto-tuned rock music sung by teenaged artists filled the room. *Yo Got Skank* by The Buttly Boys was currently playing.

Clowns patrolled the aisles with free samples for the little ones. Large signs touted remedies that cured your new conditions instigated by your previous remedies for your previous conditions. We immediately picked up two bottles of Super Leg Pro and dropped them into our burgeoning cart. It felt magical.

It was a great deal as well. Only ninety five dollars for a twin pack with ten pills in each pack.

"Maybe we should read the label first, just to be sure there are no possible reactions to the other fifty pills that we take every day," my wife suggested.

"Let's see," I responded, looking at the label. "Do not take with food, water, air, other pills, alcohol, party wieners, or Viagra. If symptoms of vomiting, convulsions, exploding organs, or bleeding orifices persist, stop taking Super Leg Pro immediately. If death occurs call your doctor or next of kin."

"Sounds safe to me. There! I think my leg just twitched." she said, and took a pill on the spot.

We headed for the checkout counter, pulling our frequent swallower coupons from our wallets.

Heart

Take this simple test. Put one of your hands, with fingers extended, on your wrist. Can you feel anything? Anything at all? If not, don't be concerned. It's perfectly natural. However, please ask someone else to confirm your findings at your earliest convenience.

Vision

Can You See This?

We didn't think so.

Joints

The one on the corner has dollar beer for happy hour - no - just kidding. Touch your toes. Do it now. Grunting and groaning is not only accepted but insisted upon. What's that? Oh, I see. Well, thanks for trying anyway.

Brain/Memory

Remember the time that you found the hundred dollar bill and I hid it for you so you could use it when you really needed it? No? Then, never mind.

Skin/Hair

There are whole industries out there waiting to address all of your skin and hair issues. Because of that, and the fact that discussing your skin and hair kind of makes us want to spit up a little bit, you are on your own for this particular situation. Good luck.

Prostate

For the men out there, be aware that if you have to pee every half hour, but can't actually do it when it is time, then you probably have a prostate gland. We're sorry.

Weight/Stomach

Can you see your feet? We didn't think so. Remember though, it says on the internet that a bit of extra weight adds years to your life. And our friends who own the local *all you can eat* place have confirmed it.

Running/Jumping/Ladders

Don't.

Signs that You are Getting Older

- You recognize the four horsemen of the apocalypse and realize that you went to school with them.

- Nursing home residents call you Gramps.

- People with walkers offer to help you across the street.

- Medics randomly begin performing CPR on you.

- Your spouse gets unsolicited mailers from funeral homes that say you have been pre-selected.

- You find yourself at a bus stop in Brooklyn wearing a Dodgers uniform.

- You find some clay tablets in your closet, and remember that some of them were correspondence from your friend Hectorus Flavious in college.

- Although you can't remember agreeing to do it, you see a huge smiling image of your face on a billboard featuring that new hemorrhoid ointment *Rear Guard*.

- The nursing home says that you qualify for a senior discount.

- Depends sends you a frequent flyer award and unexpectedly names you to their board of directors.

- Your children just went onto social security, at the full acceptance date.

Getting old is something that should not be feared or loathed. It should be invoked as a rite of passage, although you haven't actually passed yet.

Consider that, after all those things you did in college, and that trip to Central America in the brightly painted minivan, it is a wonder that you are still alive at all.

When our children and grandchildren visit these days, it warms our hearts to know that we are an important part of the reason that they are smart, resourceful individuals, who are succeeding in the world. We are sure that the allergies and bad teeth are just a coincidence.

Take pride in your age. Take heart in the idea that someone out there may possibly believe that the world is a better place with you in it. And consider that being here is far better than the alternative.

As Boomers, we are reminded of the times when we were hopeful, energetic, and proud to be alive. The times when we experienced all of those things that people do: falling in love, having a family, having a family with someone who you actually married, getting sued, eating sushi, that first trip to the emergency room, almost voting, and many other things as well.

We really mean it when we say that each and every Boomer out there makes this world a better place. Embrace your age. Cherish it. Love it. Live it.

Your legacy stands right before you, little finger in his nose at the moment. Never forget that your children and grandchildren are nothing less than your honored heritage, and real immortality. You will always be remembered.

Age gracefully. You deserve it.

38

I See Dead People

Terdlok was the village shaman. He had striking blond hair and blue eyes. Some say it was why he got the job. All the other men in the tribe had dark hair and brown eyes.

No one was really sure how he had come to look like he did. He had arrived in the village a few years back in the middle of the night, panting and out of breath, as if he were being chased.

The next day he had already acquired one of the better huts and had installed a sign by the front door stating that *The Doctor is In,* written in the local dialect.

Currently, Terdlok was huddled in the topmost branches of an ancient banyan tree in the middle of the village square. He had been there for quite some time now. This particular tree was sacred to the tribe, long known as The Tree of Life.

By his reckoning the sun had risen and set three times already and was preparing to rise once again. He had been driven to this specific location as a last resort due to an unpleasant situation that continued to unfold.

He recalled being chased relentlessly by forty or fifty of the village warriors. They were clearly angry at him for one reason or another. He considered the possibility that there may be some connection with his work related activities.

He had established an ongoing program of counseling

and advising all the young women of the tribe privately, in sessions he described as massage therapy.

Just before the chase began, another young female villager had given birth to the latest new member of the tribe. The fact that the child had the same bright yellow hair, blue eyes, and specific facial features that only the shaman possessed, may have exacerbated this evolving incident. It was the third child born this month with similar, unique physical attributes, certainly just another coincidence.

The threatening crowd was getting larger. As the shouting group waved their arms with determined gestures, it appeared that one small team was assembling a collection of branches and leaves around the base of the tree.

It would be a shame to see this sacred landmark burn down now after having been the cornerstone of their culture for hundreds of years. However, the warriors lighting the torches appeared to disagree with that assessment at the moment.

Clouds had been gathering over the area for the last few hours. Terdlok could see them moving in from the South from his special vantage point.

Suddenly, the rain began in earnest. In this part of the world the volume of water produced during a storm could really be spectacular, and this was another one of those times.

The warrior's torches sputtered and the flames went out. The entire village ran to the huge cave that had protected them from this type of thunder storm for many generations.

In short order, the shaman climbed down from the top of the tree and entered his finely appointed hut. Since he had been expecting a possible pushback to his therapeutic techniques, he had made some minor preparations. He knew that when the villagers emerged from the cave they would have forgotten all about the incident. Stocking the cave with barrels of fermented fern wine had been one of his better ideas.

He glanced at the crude village calendar hanging on the wall showing all the important dates and ceremonies. Hmmm, he mused. Today is father's day.

A blond child peered into the hut, having just emerged from the cave. *Cute kid,* the shaman briefly noted.

Eventually Terdlock died. However, his legacy lived on, as he ultimately became the founding father of Sweden.

Several hundred or so generations later, genealogy was invented to help family members search for valued ancestors, usually initiated for the primary purposes of borrowing money, starting a lawsuit, or seeking an inheritance from one deceased relative or another.

In this regard we have prepared a comprehensive primer on the subject. Let's start with a few basics:

It Begins

It was a Friday morning like any other. The mail had just arrived. We knew this because, once again, the dog raced around and howled as if we were being invaded by Liechtenstein. The dog escaped once again when we opened the door to get the mail. The mailman has since applied for a change of routes, but that's another story.

As it turned out, it was actually a FedEx truck that had

made a rare delivery to our house. The envelope was fat and looked important. In fact, it was a special delivery.

When my wife opened the envelope, our hopes of being found as a lost heir to a fortune, which was also our primary retirement income strategy, were finally being answered. In fact, the first sentence on the letter, typed on ivory colored linen stock, read, "You may be an heir of a recently deceased relative..."

Wait just a darn minute, I pondered. *These solicitations all come from someplace in Nigeria. It must be a fake.* I was hesitant to read further because the words "A legal action has been initiated in your name" appeared on the page. But curiosity (greed) caused me to continue.

It was a letter from a law firm in Utah proclaiming that we were one of many potential heirs to a single individual who had died without a will, somewhere in Michigan. It was beginning to get interesting.

Wait just a darn minute, I pondered again. *This can't be real.* So my wife called the attorney involved, and sure enough, this was a legitimate probate case to which we were a party. We were going to be rich.

Reality is a Bitch

The lawyer advised us that there were indeed a significant number of potential heirs involved in this situation, but that it was definitely worth our while to sign the ninety page form, written in six point type.

"Our firm only retains seventy five percent of your inheritance for our services," the document confirmed.

"Sounds reasonable," I enthusiastically agreed. And we quickly signed and returned the form.

The actions we then took can only be described as surreal. We prepared to hire a real estate agent in the Bahamas, a pastry chef, an aroma therapist, and a team of pet iguana handlers.

As part of our evolving due diligence my wife agreed to become our formal family tree researcher for the project.

It was not her first sortie into the genealogy world. Sometime in the past she had received some documents and pictures from various relatives describing the lives and activities of some of our ancestors.

Her previous work revealed that we also appear to be related to Santa, Attila the Hun, and some guy named Terdlock.

This time, however, it was more than just musing about how our DNA could be blamed for the many failures and bad habits that we had developed over the years.

Great Aunt Mehitabel had indeed indulged a bit as noted in the 1930 census, but this time we needed more data...a lot more.

The software was purchased, the boxes of letters and pictures removed from the attic, and the designated work area was isolated. Our house quickly became overwhelmed in piles of paper and other flammable materials.

In time, the truth began to be revealed. There were hundreds of cousins, aunts, uncles, grandmothers, and other types of relatives who were also in line for a portion of the inheritance.

And sadly, most of them were still alive. One relative was found to be well over one hundred and actively participating in mixed martial arts somewhere in New England. Our hopes were dashed.

Too bad the down payment on the Lear Jet had already been cashed by the bank.

In the end, we abandoned any hope of receiving an unexpected inheritance. The good news is that now my wife is a legitimate expert in genealogy. She has been contacted by several diverse political organizations to unearth dirt on their opponents, and business has been good.

To help deflect any potential unexpected discoveries by one of your family members who has decided to research your family tree details, we offer this valuable unsolicited advice:

Important Genealogy Facts

- Genealogy is different than geology, or so they tell me.

- Yes, you have ancestors. Many of them went to prison.

- The size of your house does not matter when researching your ancestry. Every square inch will be covered in musty documents, flip charts, sticky notes, and very old pictures (some in frames) when the process begins. We lost our pet pygmy pig last week. However, I am sure Flipper is still here somewhere. I thought I heard whimpering last night.

- Most of your ancestors had unpronounceable or simply ridiculous names. Experts are still not sure why.

- You will never actually talk to your in-house genealogist again in person, unless you die.

- Your family tree is really important. Our relatives once planted a mighty sequoia as a living symbol of family strength and continuity, but its stump is now under a Burger King parking lot.

- One day you may get a notice from a lawyer saying that you might be in line for a portion of an unknown ancestor's large inheritance. In every case you will be just below the cut-off line and receive nothing but a bill from the lawyer. In very rare cases you might actually receive a tiny check in the mail that will buy a cup at Starbuck's (not the coffee, just the cup).

- All of your deceased relatives were in the military at some point. Many were front line fighters for countries that no longer exist, such as Texas.

- Contacting your living relatives to help in your genealogical research will always result in sudden visits or having children left in the night on your door step. We urge caution.

You Have a History

Thanks to technology, we live in a unique time in history that allows all of us to effectively explore our relatives' most intimate and depraved histories in great detail.

Information is now available, at a price, for exploring your family history all the way back to your twenty-times ago great uncle who ran a self service dinosaur wash.

For Boomers, it actually wasn't that many generations ago that our grandparents made that treacherous journey across the ocean to America, and the even more dangerous journey down the gang plank and into town.

Some family histories are quite fascinating. Our personal ancestry ties us to the inventor of the Ocarina, and even further back, to a failed toga broker in Ancient Greece.

It makes perfect sense for each of us to aspire to learn about our ancestry. In fact, we just learned that another of our distant relatives from upstate Mississippi, who apparently ran something called a gator and tarantula ranch, just died.

The letter says that the inheritance is to be paid by relocating large quantities of the current livestock inventory to each qualifying heir's garage.

Cha-Ching...maybe.

39

How to Live Forever

The baby mastodon was so cute. It tried to stand in the specially designed incubator, but just couldn't make it work. Honks of frustration filled the room as the small beast bounced around the enclosure. It almost sounded like swearing.

Of course, if he had a mother to help with the process it would have been much easier to manage, and he certainly would have been reprimanded for cursing. But the last mother of his species had died many thousands of years ago.

The genetics lab was situated deep in the heart of a mountain in North Dakota. The government agencies and scientists involved had seen all of the Jurassic Park movies, and didn't want any of their on-purpose or accidental hundred foot tall intelligent killer carnivores escaping into downtown Bismarck.

This situation was in fact the first of its kind. Cloning had been successful on many kinds of animals and their microscopic relatives, but never before on an extinct species, and the experiment was going well so far.

In short order the young, previously extinct beast figured out how to move freely around its enclosure.

He (yes - he - they turned him over to check) presently stood and headed immediately for the food trough located in the far corner.

Suddenly, little Barnabas (the mastodon's new name,

selected by charging thousands of contestants to possibly win a diesel Volkswagen), looked up at the gallery of onlookers seated safely above the large cage.

"Excuse me," said the creature in a passable English accent. "Do you happen to know where they keep the salt?"

The events that occurred after that historical interchange are a long story that must be saved for discussion another day.

The point is of course, that cloning is about to be accomplished in a world-changing way...

...and that means pretty soon they can and will be able to clone YOU!

Growing old gracefully

Until Medicare adds cloning to your plan (presumably only as a complex, indecipherable, supplemental option like all other actually needed procedures, of course), you may have to contemplate living out the rest of your life with your current body.

With this in mind, there are a few things that you can do to live healthier, happier, longer, and occasionally even sober.

In fact, there are four key components to enjoying a longer life:

1. Nutrition

What you eat is important. You may have been told this before, but after a certain age it actually is something that you may want stop challenging by eating and drinking, well, basically nothing but crap.

First let's discuss the four basic food groups:

- Cabernet
- Merlot
- Chardonnay
- Cheese

Yes, we realize there may be other foods that could be considered valuable in your diet, such as potato chips, olives, and pork rinds, but for the best health results stick with the basics and eat only these approved foods.

2. Lifestyle

The key elements for determining your lifestyle choices involve drinking, smoking, over-eating, chewing gum, and chewing your own gums.

All drinkers understand the clear, positive benefits of riboflavin and solenoids found in all wines. Some wines even include stems, cork, and bits of foil, all known to be helpful for maintaining proper fiber and mineral levels within the body.

Smokers know that it is going to kill them relatively quickly, but just don't care. Or maybe that is why they do it. Don't smoke.

All over-eaters should chew gum instead, and stop chewing your gums. Now!

Gambling/Taxes

Many/most/all Boomers gamble. Most do it at casinos, but many also do it on their taxes. Our advice is simply to not gamble more than you can afford to lose in the parking lot if you drop it. And pay your taxes, or at least some of them, after taking the understandable deductions for your Alpaca farm in Iceland that is obviously losing money.

Attitude

Have one. Have a good one. For example, say to yourself "I feel really good that I can still see my feet," or "Yes, I ate it all including the wrapper. So what?"

Intimacy

The dictionary defines intimacy as a state marked by emotional closeness. You probably expected this section to have something or other to do with maintaining a healthy sexual relationship, but we all know that ship sailed a long time ago. In practice, get a pet, or one of those Japanese blow-up pillows shaped like a frog, for companionship.

3. Genetics/Environment

Family Tree

We all have one. Ours is a monkey pod. This relates closely with the dumb luck segment (see below). If you happened to have been born into a rich, loving, smart, thoughtful, or lucky family, good for you. For the rest of us, make the most of whatever genetics you have been given. Legs are always a plus.

Smog

Everyone knows that smog is going to kill us all, and soon. We suggest moving to Beijing or Mexico City to get it over with more quickly.

Internet

Thankfully the internet will solve everything for all of us, including smog. For the few of you who have not done it yet, get your Facebook page set up immediately. Start a specialty group tied to your key interests, such as raising poisonous reptiles or refining weapons grade uranium. Seek out small animals, take their picture(s) doing something adorable, such as biting the mailman, and post it on YouTube. This can all be monetized, and you'll never need to work again.

Dust Mites

The dust mite problem is even worse now than it used to be. Today those balls of fuzzy things in every corner and under every object in your house are full blown mite colonies. You may as well stop trying to remove them with your Dyson, although it has been proven that the Dyson does kill many of them, along with your pets. In regards to the mites, simply understand that it is already too late. Sorry.

4. Dumb Luck (Good/Bad)

Asteroids/Meteorite Strikes/Dental Plaque

The next asteroid strike will occur a week from Friday. Meteor strikes happen thousands of time a day, and your best hope is that one of them doesn't hit you while waiting for the light to change. Excessive dental plaque will probably get you in any case. We hope this helps.

Winning the Lottery/Losing the Ticket

You read every day about the person who won the lottery and then won it again a week later. You also read about someone who swears they won the lottery but lost the ticket or had it stolen by their next door neighbor's dog. If you buy the winning ticket, we suggest that you don't lose it.

Pre-Cloning Suggestions for a Longer Life

- Remind your grandchildren that, although you haven't seen any of the Jurassic Park movies, you were alive during the actual Jurassic and got to see the dinosaurs first hand. In fact, you had a pet one named Ralph.

- When someone tries to help you stand up, let them, unless you are already standing.

- Be sure to use your senior citizen discount when participating in class five rock climbing and white water rapids kayaking events.

- With your artificial hip, you should stop attending sit-ins, bra burnings, and naked drum ceremonies. Remember that if you sit, you won't be able to get back up.

- Limit your naps to six or seven hours. You can make up the critical time for resting by going to bed a few hours early each night.

- Consider trying Preparation G instead of the more popular and expensive Preparation H. Except for the superficial burns, seizures, and festering boils with the G, they work pretty much the same.

- Don't let being banned from the local all you can eat restaurant for going back for the snow crab legs twenty times in one visit bother you. They are delicious.

- Play some video games with the grandkids. We have heard that your Donkey Kong scores are legendary.

In the end, your legacy and immortality reside with the children and grandchildren. The fact that most of them are on the run, in a cult, or in prison is incidental.

Maybe one of your progeny will produce or create something that will change the world, like the pet rock or Kleenex.

It is even possible that someday in the not too distant future, your grandson or granddaughter will perfect the cloning process...and make a new you. Amazingly, it actually might happen.

40

Simpler Times

In the beginning things were very simple indeed:

See food!
( ) Hit with rock
( ) Hit with stick

And for many years after that, life was still much simpler than it is today. For example, if you lived on a farm the decision making process went something like this:

Is the cow sick?
( ) Yes
( ) No

Is it raining?
( ) Yes
( ) No

Where is my daughter?
( ) House
( ) Barn

Where is the cowhand?
( ) Barn
( ) Anywhere else

Then, with early technology, things began to get a bit more complicated:

What should we watch on television?
( ) Ed Sullivan
( ) Lawrence Welk

The car won't start. What should I check?
( ) Gas
( ) Battery

What should we have for dinner?
( ) Hot Dogs
( ) Hamburgers

And then things began to get really complicated with the invention of the PC and cell phone:

Did you plug it in?
( ) Yes
( ) No

Can you hear me now?
( ) Yes
( ) No
( ) You're breaking up

Did you back up your completed doctoral dissertation before spilling coffee on your floppy disk?
( ) Yes
( ) No

Today however, things are not simple at all, or at least they wouldn't be without the internet.

BTW, you'll need to learn the meaning of OMG and WFT, along with several other letters.

And thanks to the internet, most of mankind's pressing questions can now be answered with a few key strokes, such as:

Is Pluto a planet?

Does a McRib contain any actual meat?

Which are God's favorite boy bands?

Etc.

There is even a theory that, in the near future children will be implanted with a cell phone like device at birth and will be given their own ring tone. But this may not actually happen for a few more months.

It is our unrealistic belief that we are nearing a cultural technology revolution in which people will finally shout "ENOUGH!" and begin the transition back to simpler times.

At first, people will stop tweeting for a few minutes a day.

Then the day will come when someone leaves their cell phone at home by accident and doesn't immediately drive six hours back from their failing grandmother's bedside to get it.

And finally, one day in the distant future, a child will be asked to read a book again at school.

As the future unfolds, there is hope that we may return to truly simpler times - times when things that were really important in the world become important again. Things like, "When I get my hands on that dang cowhand..."

We can only dream.

41

Ever After

It was a Tuesday in April, and still unbelievably cold outside. The winter season was waning, but still fully in play.

Soon the other season, road construction, would begin, and it would be blazing hot for months on end. But that was weeks away. After all, this was the Midwest.

At this time of year, most people were preparing to un-install the snow blades from the front of their pickup trucks, that they had put on last winter as required by law here.

The local Boomer population had survived another year, making many new friends and acquaintances, acquiring the next dog or ferret, and mowing the lawn three times a week.

Life was good for the nearly and newly retired.

There was always plenty to do here in every season, of course. In fact, another barely planned *do something in a group while drinking* event was about to begin.

A large contingent of Boomers descended on the local watering hole like falcons on a field mouse. One of the bartenders looked up and muttered, "Here comes the Out to Pasture Posse again."

It was trivia night.

There were big bowls of various snack foods scattered

around the room among the pool tables. The meatballs in particular, were popular with the group that had gathered for the soon to be epic competition involving trivia featuring farm animals.

One of the contestants shouted, "The bartender found some meatballs way in the back of the walk-in cooler with the expiration dates smudged off. They are letting them go at half price! Except for the green part, they taste okay to me."

All had agreed that Hoyle's Rules for Unimportant and Marginally Factual Trivia would be the order of the day. There was to be no biting, kicking, general disemboweling, or eye poking. There were to be no death threats or related activities.

The multi-page contracts releasing the establishment of any form of liability for any reason forever were about to be signed in triplicate by all contestants.

So, naturally someone immediately got poked in the eye during the distribution of the trivia response button sets. It seemed that one of the teams, who had named themselves the Take No Prisoners, really wanted to play using the unit with the blue buttons.

The competition commenced and lasted nearly until dawn.

The first prize, a large bag of past pull date Snickers Bars and Skittles, was won by the usual winning team, the Why Do the Rest of You Even Bother's.

They had worn their sparkly Elvis suits with sunglasses, and had prevailed in the tie breaker at the end of the game (something involving raccoons).

After the usual official challenge regarding an apparent Googling, and the subsequent near disemboweling, the winners took their rightful place on the reviewing stand (the bar top).

The rest of the group had wandered off to the front of the bar and had taken up the new challenge of determining the correct spelling and pronunciation of Jagermeister, and the more important related question, how many shots does it take to see Heaven?

The answer is apparently twelve.

Eventually, the group of friends disbursed. Some of them were even able to find their cars, and presumably their way home.

Everyone agreed that the night had once again indeed been...epic.

On Being a Boomer

It is understood that you were certainly expecting to have experienced even one pithy, life changing epiphany from this guide. You had at least counted on some take-aways.

After all, it has been your loyal and faithful literary companion during the entire twenty minutes or so that it most likely took you to pretend that you were reading the chapters.

Well then, think about this for a minute. As a Boomer, you are getting relentlessly older. There is nothing you can do about it. Generations X, Y, Z, and a bunch of, twenty-something kids called Millennials, who all apparently ask continuously to be promoted every couple of weeks, are running around all over the place.

As a Boomer, you will never understand why they keep making television programs that feature somebody's living room filled with many of those previously noted generationals, fighting with each other over a candy bar.

Your children have all grown up, and except for the fact that they have moved back in with you along with their children, pets, and a few other people that they apparently know, you are living in an empty nest.

And even though you unfortunately wished that you could have learned to dance hip-hop at some point, you thankfully didn't.

Someday, when there are flying cars, little glowing cubes of greenish gelatin for food, and telephones that don't need cords, you may even die.

So here is your take-away. As an official Boomer, isn't it just about time to go out there and have a little fun?

You're welcome.

What It Really Means

What does it mean to be a Boomer? It means far more than being an inadvertent participant in a post-war population increase in America. Every Boomer has a story to tell.

All Boomers have lived through personal and national times of great promise and joy, and of even greater loss and heartbreak.

Think about this sometime. Every Boomer has changed the world, and continues to do so. We are proud that you are one of them. May each of you live happily ever after.

The Boomer's Code

- Always be true to yourself, and your ferret.

- Life is too short for cheap wine, except during happy hour.

- Your bucket list must not include the use of any actual buckets.

- What would the Beatles do?

- You can never own too many trampolines.

Appendix

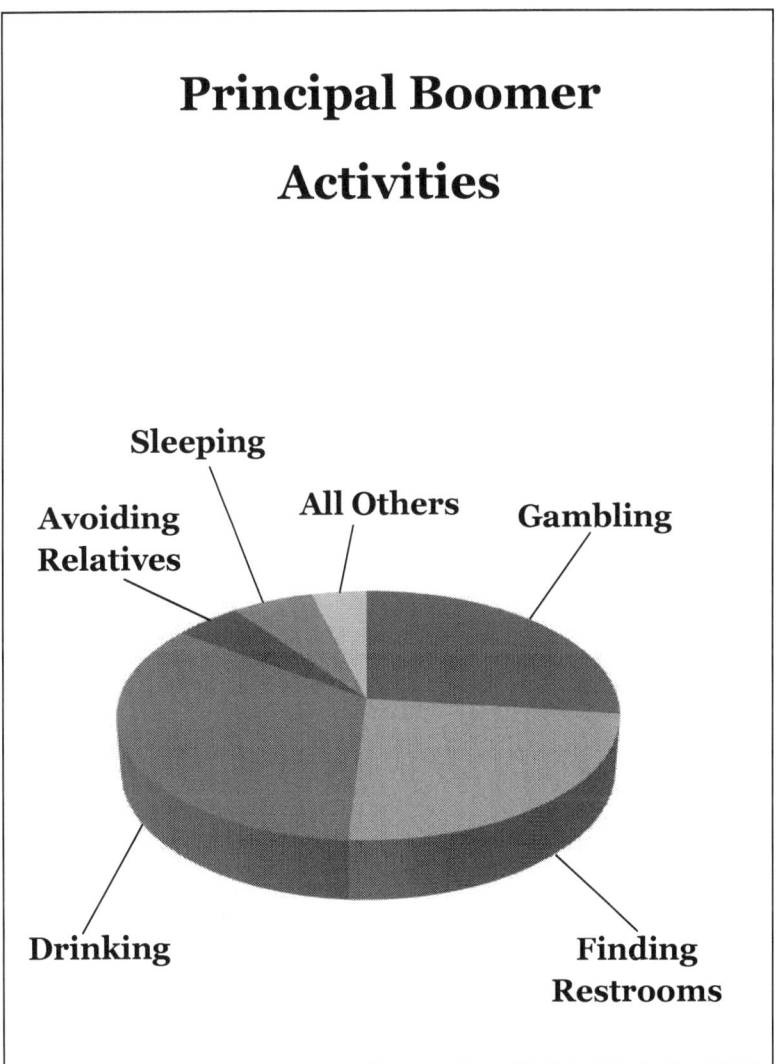

About the Author

Terry spent over thirty years in the corporate world performing a variety of tasks, including managing large numbers of reluctant and often confused employees, and collating different colored sheets of paper, at which he excelled.

Having lived a very long time at this point, and being an official member of the *Boomer Population*, he feels uniquely qualified to advise all other Boomers in the art and science of living out their few remaining years.

The author currently lives in a small town in the Midwest with his wife and no dogs. It is a long story how this came to be and we won't bother you with the details. However, living nearby are some of his kids, their kids, some dogs, and a few small fish. He has some other kids as well, but they don't live here.

Terry used to live in a major metropolitan area that included large buildings, several politicians, and a sports team, but he can't remember exactly where.

When not writing guidebooks, Terry gets the mail several times a month, and occasionally mows part of the lawn.

Made in the USA
Columbia, SC
02 July 2017